Picture credits

p14   © I.W.M. – "The Trustees of the I.W.M. London"

p15   Peter Newark's Military Pictures

p18   The Bridgeman Art Library, London/Private Collection

p19   Hulton Getty Picture Collection

p22   E.T. archive

p23   Will Dyson, *The Daily Herald* (13.05.1919), Centre for the Study of Cartoons and Caricature, University of Kent, Canterbury

p26   Leonard Raven Hill, *Punch* (10.12.1919), Centre for the Study of Cartoons and Caricature, University of Kent, Canterbury, © *Punch*

p27   David Low, *Star* (24.11.1932), Centre for the Study of Cartoons and Caricature, University of Kent, Canterbury, © Solo Syndication

p30   David Low, *Evening Standard*, Centre for the Study of Cartoons and Caricature, University of Kent, Canterbury, © Solo Syndication

p31   *Punch*

p34   Novosti (London)

p38   Novosti (London)

p39   David King Collection

p50   AKG London

p51   Ullstein Bilderdienst

p54   Walker Evans, © Hulton Deutsch Collection Limited

p58   © Colombus Dispatch, Ohio

p59   *Punch*

p62   *(left)* AKG London, *(right) Punch*

p63   David Low, © Solo Syndication

p67   David King Collection

p70   © I.W.M. – "The Trustees of the I.W.M. London"

p78   Cliché J.-L. Charmet

p82   David King Collection

p91   *(left) The Philadelphia Courier*, *(right)* Associated Press Photo

Published by BBC Educational Publishing, BBC White City, 201 Wood Lane, London W12 7TS

First published 1998, Reprinted 1999 (twice)
© Allan Todd/BBC Worldwide (Educational Publishing) 1998

ISBN: 0 563 46122 5

Designed by Sally Fentiman
Printed in Great Britain by Bell & Bain, Glasgow

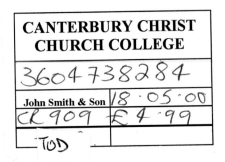

History

Modern World History

Allan Todd

(Senior Examiner, GCSE Modern European and World History)

Contents

6

About BITESIZEhistory

BITESIZEhistory is a revision guide that has been specially put together to help you with your GCSE exams. You can tape the TV programmes and watch them on video, work your way through the activities and suggestions in this book, and even dial up the Internet on-line service.

It's called BITESIZEhistory because it's been divided up into manageable bitesize pieces of revision – much better than doing hours of revision the day before your exam! The video programmes, which give you information and advice, can be watched as often as you want until you have grasped all the points. Many video sections tie in with units in the book, which is divided into small sections that you can work through one by one. If you still don't understand something, you can contact the on-line team who are there to help you.

How to use this book

This book is divided into seven sections, sub-divided into units, which cover the key GCSE topics of Modern World History. If you have any doubts about which topics you need to cover, ask your teacher.

Each unit of the book follows the same pattern:

- an introduction page which lists all the main areas you need to know about the topic. It also tells you what particular type of question you'll be practising, and the two mini-topics the questions will be based on

- a Factzone page, which gives more detailed historical information about the two mini-topics to be dealt with

- two pages of exam-type questions on those two mini-topics – one example question, with tips to help you understand what the examiner is looking for; and one practice question (also with reminders and hints to help you understand more clearly what the question is asking you to do).

For many of the units, there are corresponding sections on the video. In such cases, it's a good idea to watch the video sequence(s) *after* reading the Factzone page, but *before* you try to work through or answer one of the questions. This is because the video sequences give you extra information and tips on how to answer exam questions. It's also a good idea to write the time-codes from the video on the relevant page(s) of the book – this will help you find the video sequences quickly, as you go over units again.

The most important sections of the GCSE Modern World History syllabus (regardless of exam board) are covered by the book – but BITESIZEhistory doesn't aim to give total coverage of all topics. So it's important to carry on using your school textbook and your own notes. Because all the main types of GCSE History questions are covered, the general tips and suggestions will be

KEY TO SYMBOLS

📺 A link to the video

❓ Something to think about

◎ An activity to do

useful, even if some of your specific topics do not appear in the BITESIZEhistory book. Remember, the skills are transferable to the content of any topic.

The activities suggested in the book include:

■ highlighting (either with highlighter pens, or by underlining or circling) certain bits in the sources and/or in the origin details which accompany the sources (i.e. the information about the sources provided by the Chief Examiner, such as date, country of origin, who wrote, produced or photographed it). This activity makes you look closely at the sources and their details of origin. It's something you could usefully do on your final exam papers, to make sure you don't miss any points

■ writing – either short-answer questions of one or two sentences, or more extended writing of several paragraphs or essays.

Taken together, the book and the video cover all the main skills required in GCSE History.

How to revise for GCSE History

There are three main aspects to successful revision, as opposed to unplanned, unfocused and therefore unsuccessful revision! These are:

■ **organise:** prepare a long-term revision plan, in order to make the most of your time

■ **learn:** make sure you know the relevant facts

■ **apply:** understand and practise how to answer different types of questions.

Organise

You need to draw up a revision timetable to cover all your subjects – not just History! It should begin three or four months (not days!) before your exams start. Perhaps your school produces one – you could use that, or adapt it to suit your own needs. Once you've drawn up an outline timetable, divide the days (say, 90 or 100) by the number of subjects you're taking. This will tell you how many days you've got for revising History. Three very important things about revision are:

1 Don't try to revise for more than about 40 minutes at a time, otherwise you may overload your brain! About three 40-minute sessions per night is enough for most people. Make sure your plan includes breaks (of at least 10–15 minutes) between each session. If you are revising hard, you'll need to take short breaks.

2 Be realistic – build in time off as well for activities like the cinema, sport or parties. One complete day off and one night off a week is reasonable. If you start early enough and you revise hard, you should be able to persuade your parents that some time off is okay!

THE ON-LINE SERVICE
You can find extra support, tips and answers to your exam queries on the BITESIZE Internet site. The address is http://www.bbc.co.uk/education/revision

3 Try to stick to your plan. If illness, for example, disrupts it, try to re-organise your plan to take account of this. Again, if you start early enough, you can get round problems like this without panicking.

Learn

This is much harder – and less pleasant! – than drawing up a revision timetable. First of all, make sure that you know the exam requirements (such as topics, and the number and type of exam papers). If necessary, check with your teacher.

Instead of rewriting your notes several times over, or simply re-reading your textbook, try some other revision methods:

- **highlight** or underline key terms and facts in your notes
- write these key points briefly on to **index cards**
- draw **spider diagrams**
- listen to **tape recordings** of you (or a friend or parent) reading out the main points
- ask someone to **test you** on a topic
- make **visual displays** of the main points of a unit on A4 or A3 paper, with brief facts in boxes, as in this example:

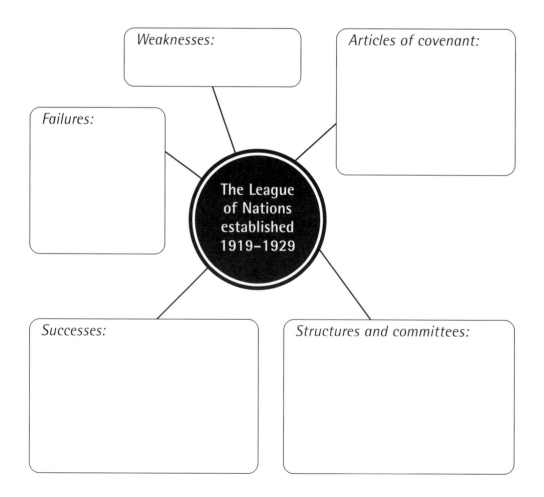

These diagrams can then be highlighted or underlined to help your memory. Then put them up on your bedroom wall. You should be able to cover most topics in four or five pages at most.

Whatever methods you adopt, make sure you work in a quiet, warm room away from distractions. Try to keep your revision varied. For example, use a combination of note-making on cards, highlighting, writing fuller notes, and doing practice questions.

Apply

It's as important to practise answering the different types of questions as it is to learn the facts. For one History revision session, you could read through the Factzone on a topic, watch the video sequence (if there is one), and then work through the example question. In your next revision session you could read through the second part of the Factzone, watch any video sequence, and then do the practice question – making sure you follow the Remember points and the Think suggestions.

In particular, make sure that you look at and work through the full variety of questions, which range from:

- **short-answer source comprehension/understanding questions** – which simply ask you to pick out bits of information from a source

- **short-answer comprehension in context questions** – which require you to add facts from your own knowledge to the information given by a source or to explain a term and its significance

- **source usefulness/source reliability questions** – both types require you to talk about a source and its provenance/origin details as regards:

  1 nature/type: Is it primary or secondary? Was it written for a private or public audience? Is it a diary entry, or an official document?

  2 author: Was it written/taken by someone in a position to know? Or is it likely to be biased? Or is it by someone (a historian, for example) who has done wide, and probably objective, research?

  3 purpose: Was it written/taken in order to influence people (such as propaganda)? Or was it intended to be accurate (such as a report)?

  4 typicality: Is the source representative/typical of people's thoughts or a particular situation? Or is it just a limited view of one person, time or place?

Remember, even a biased or unreliable source can be useful, for example as evidence of how people thought, or as an example of propaganda. (Make sure you spell "bias" and "biased" correctly!)

- **source comparison/cross-referencing questions** – which require you to show how one source agrees and disagrees with another. The examiner is not trying to catch you out, so both sources will have differences as well as similarities

- **source sufficiency questions** – which ask you to write about some historical situation, using the information provided by several sources and your own knowledge. Make sure that you say something about all the sources and that you add some of the facts you have remembered. If you only write about the sources or your own knowledge, you'll lose half the marks available

- **extended writing questions** – either one or two paragraph questions, or essay questions, which require you to structure the facts you have revised into a logical, planned piece of writing. This is especially important for essays. For "why" type essay questions in particular, make sure you don't just write down everything you know. Instead, select and use only the facts relevant to the question. Always try to do a concluding/summary paragraph.

Finally, if some topics you're revising for the exam aren't in the book, or your particular topics are in the book but don't give you practice of all the types of questions above, don't panic. Look at the types of questions not covered, regardless of topic. The skills and tips are transferable to any topic.

On the day

Make sure you know which sections you have been prepared for. If in doubt, ask before the exam has started! Note carefully the total time available, and sort out the time you'll spend on each question, giving more time to those questions carrying the highest marks.

If there is a choice of questions, read through each one carefully, to ensure you choose the one(s) you know most about. For an essay question, make a rough plan first – it helps you find out right at the beginning whether you know enough about the topic (if you don't, it gives you time to select another!). It also gives you something to jot down in the last few minutes should you get into serious time trouble – you will get some marks for a note-style answer.

Finally, don't panic! If you have followed your teacher's advice and the suggestions in this book, you will be well-prepared for any question the Chief Examiner can think up. And remember, the exam is not meant to catch you out: it is designed to let you show what you know, understand and can do.

Now read on...

Good luck!

Revision notes

You can write notes here about the topics you have revised and those you still need to revise.

12

To be able to answer questions on this topic, you will need to know about the following:

• the Schlieffen Plan
(invasion of Belgium, British Expeditionary Force)

• the Western Front
(Ypres 1915; Verdun, the Somme 1916; Passchendaele1917)

• trench warfare
(dreadful conditions: mud, frostbite, rats, typhus-bearing lice. Heavy shelling and poison gas attacks led to "shell shock" and even desertions and mutinies)

• the other Fronts
(Eastern, Balkan, Italian, Middle Eastern)

• the war at sea
(Jutland, submarines)

• war in the Colonies

• stalemate on the Western Front
(several major battles but no significant breakthrough. Millions of casualties for advances of a few kilometres)

• new technology and tactics
(gas, tanks, convoys, Zeppelins, planes)

• entry of USA into the war

• Allied naval blockade of German ports

This section deals with the fighting on the Western Front, focusing on:

■ the trenches

■ new technology and tactics

It also gives you practice at short-answer questions which test source comprehension in context. For questions like this, you need to use your own knowledge of the topic to understand and explain a particular term, point, feature or comment in a source, and explain its wider historical background or significance.

The trenches

Sept 1914   The German advance was pushed back at the Battle of the Marne. Both sides began to dig trenches and fast military movements came to an end.

Oct 1914   Both sides were involved in the **race for the sea** (rush to capture Channel ports).

Nov 1914   By the end of month, both sides were "dug in" for winter in a complex pattern of zig-zag trenches, 470 km long, from the North Sea to Switzerland.

Trenches   There were four types: reserve, support, communication, front line. They were defended/reinforced by machine-guns and barbed wire. Attacks began with heavy shelling of enemy trenches (to kill defenders and destroy barbed wire). Then attacking troops advanced (**going over the top**) across **no-man's land** (ground between the two opposing front lines, controlled by neither side).

Nov 1915 – Dec 1917   Stalemate on Western Front and **war of attrition** (to win by destroying more enemy forces, even if own losses are very heavy, and so wear the other side out.)

New technolgy and tactics

Land

Gas: Poison gas (chlorine) was first used by the Germans on 22 April 1915. The victims drowned in fluid produced in their lungs. Phosgene and Mustard gas were also used by both sides. Despite the initial success, the generals remained doubtful, because the effectiveness depended on the weather. Gas masks were developed for protection.
Tanks: These were invented by the British. They were developed by the Navy in 1915 because the Army was not interested. They were first used in 1916, at the end of the Battle of the Somme. Their first serious use was at the Battle of Cambrai, in November 1917. Tanks were not used to the full until 1918.

Sea

Surface: New battleships called Dreadnoughts were developed but they fought only once, at the Battle of Jutland in 1916.
Submarines: The Germans used **U-boats**. These were a serious threat and destroyed much British **merchant shipping** (25% by April 1917). In 1917, Britain adopted new methods of countering U-boats:

■ **Hydrophones** were used to detect submarines. Depth charges were then used to destroy the submarines.

■ **Convoy system** - this was even more effective. Merchant ships sailed together in zig-zag patterns, protected by destroyers and torpedo boats. By Nov 1918, only 4% of British merchant ships were being destroyed.

Air

Planes: At first, planes were used for observation and scouting. Later they were equipped with fixed machine guns. The First World War was the first war to see sustained aerial fighting. Planes were used for bombing and attacking enemy trenches. (At first, the bombs were dropped by hand).
Airships: Germany used **Zeppelins** to bomb civilians in British cities. By 1916, British air defences (incendiary bullets, searchlights, barrage balloons as barriers, night fighters) had improved. Germany was forced to use night bombers. Zeppelins had poor navigation and found bad weather difficult. Both sides made similar technological advances, so there was no decisive breakthrough.

Short-answer source-context questions

📺 The trenches

Study the two sources below, which refer to trench warfare on the Western Front, and then answer the question which follows.

Source A Plan of a trench system.

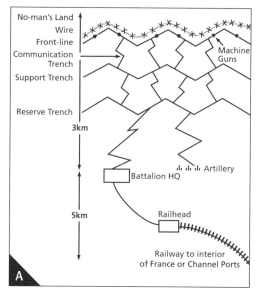

No-man's Land
Wire
Front-line
Communication Trench
Support Trench
Reserve Trench
3km
Machine Guns
Artillery
Battalion HQ
5km
Railhead
Railway to interior of France or Channel Ports
A

Source B A trench on the Western Front.

REMEMBER Short-answer source-context questions usually ask you to define a particular word, phrase or feature of a source, and to use your own knowledge to explain briefly its historical background (context).

◎ *Write one or two sentences about each of the following terms to explain their meaning:*
"no-man's land", "war of attrition" and "going over the top".

No-man's land is the land between the two front lines, which is controlled by neither side. Attacking troops had to cross through machine-gun fire, mud-filled craters, etc.

War of attrition means wearing out the enemy, by inflicting greater casualties on the enemy than are suffered by one's own troops despite heavy losses. This became the military strategy associated with trench warfare. It caused huge casualties for little gain of territory.

Going over the top means going over the top of the trenches to start an attack. It meant having to cross no-man's land to get at the enemy (usually warned by preliminary bombardment leading to heavy casualties).

New technology and tactics

Study the two sources below, which refer to the war at sea during the First World War.

Source A German U-boat

> **REMEMBER** When answering this kind of question, give a brief definition or explanation. Add some factual information to explain the history connected to the term.

B

'As the war went on, German U-boats attacked merchant ships in the Atlantic Ocean. It became necessary to form the ships into convoys for protection.'

Source B Comment on attacks on British ships.

> **REMEMBER** Check your own text book for any additional information.

Practice questions – warfare

Use sources A and B above to write one or two sentences to explain each of the following terms. Allow yourself 15 minutes to do this task.

1 U-boat

2 merchant ships

3 convoy

The Home Front

To be able to answer questions on this topic, you will need to know about the following:

• propaganda

• recruitment
(volunteers, conscription)

• opposition to war
(conscientious objectors)

• Defence of the Realm Act, 1914

• air raids
(Zeppelins and bombers)

• rationing

• the role of women
(*Work*: the large number of men at war meant new job opportunities for women but after 1918, many women lost their jobs to the returning soldiers.
Politics: before 1914, many women campaigned for the right to vote in elections – the most active were known as "suffragettes". After the war, in November 1918, women over 30 were given the right to vote. Not all historians agree that this was because of their contribution to the war effort.)

This section focuses on two aspects of the Home Front during the First World War:

■ recruitment

■ the role of women

It also gives you practice at answering questions requiring answers of one or two paragraphs. For this type of question you need to explain why something happened, or what was important. Your answer will be like a mini-essay, so you need to *think* about what you are writing, so that your answer is structured in a logical way.

You need to know this sequence of events:

Recruitment

August 1914 At the outbreak of the war, thousands of young men rushed to join the army. They were called **volunteers**. The army promised to keep volunteers from the same area, street or factory in the same regiment, which were known as **Pals Regiments.** There was massive patriotic propaganda and enthusiasm and many were attracted by the idea of excitement and glory, believing that the war would be over by Christmas.

1914–1915 The First World War became a war of trenches and attrition on the Western Front. The Government decided to build a large army. The effectiveness of propaganda and the number of volunteers lessened when people heard news about the conditions, the heavy casualties on the Front, and when the likely length of the war became apparent.

January 1916 The Military Service Act – **conscription** (compulsory military service) was introduced. At first, the law forced all single men aged 18-41 to join up. In 1918 the age was raised to 51.

March 1916 Conscription was extended to all married men. Some categories were exempted: men in **reserved occupations** (essential jobs, e.g. miners, farmers); men judged unfit; **conscientious objectors** (people opposed to all war, known as **"conchies"**). Tribunals were set up to decide who were genuine conscientious objectors – in 1916 there were over 15,000 "conchies".

The role of women

Work

The large number of men at war meant new job opportunities for women:
- as nurses or ambulance drivers at the front
- in factories which made the guns, bullets, etc (**munitions** factories). By 1918 there were over 900,000 "munitionettes"
- in other jobs traditionally done by men (drivers, ticket inspectors, etc)
- in the Women's Land Army, doing farm work
- as secretaries and clerks (500,000).

Politics

When war broke out, most women supported Britain's involvement. Some tried to get men to volunteer by giving white feathers to all young men not in uniform (sometimes, these were soldiers on leave).

Social

Before the war, women were seen as passive and home-centred. War work (e.g. as ambulance drivers and nurses, through which they shared the sufferings on the Front) and the sight of women in uniform, led to changes in:
- attitudes towards women and their roles
- fashion for women - it became more comfortable and practical (e.g. trousers)
- social freedoms (e.g. women being able to smoke and visit pubs).

One- or two-paragraph answers

⊚ Recruitment

Study the source below, which shows a British recruiting poster produced during the First World War. Answer the questions and use the notes to help.

Daddy, what did YOU do in the Great War ?

 REMEMBER To get high marks for this kind of question, don't just describe something. Show you understand what happened by using your own knowledge to explain the **causes** or the **importance** of something.

 REMEMBER Check your own textbook to see if there is any more information you could usefully add.

◎ *Write one or two paragraphs to explain why conscription was introduced in 1916.*

◎ *Write one or two paragraphs to explain why certain groups of people were allowed to avoid conscription.*

Conscription was not needed initially because of enthusiasm about the idea of a short war. By 1916, propaganda was less effective because it had become a war of attrition with heavy casualties, and a law was needed to force people to join up.

Three main groups were allowed to avoid conscription:
■ those in reserved or essential jobs because their work was vital to the war
■ those who were unfit to fight because they would be useless/a problem at the front
■ those who objected on religious or moral grounds

The role of women

Study the source below, which shows a woman bus conductor in London in 1917.

For the questions below, think about all the reasons, not just one. Check your own textbook for any additional information.

Practice questions – the Home Front

Write one or two paragraphs to answer each of the following questions. Allow yourself 25 minutes.

1 Explain why some women issued "white feathers" to young men.

2 Explain why large numbers of women became employed in a wider variety of jobs during the First World War.

3 Explain why women's status in society was changed by the war.

The Peace Treaties 1919–1923

To be able to answer questions on this topic, you will need to know about the following:

- the "Big Three" and their aims (USA, Britain, France)

- Wilson's Fourteen Points

- Treaty of Versailles, 1919 (Germany), which had eight points:

■ A **League of Nations** was set up ■ Germany was to give up land to neighbouring countries ■ All German colonies were taken away and ruled by Britain and France, under League of Nations **mandates** (permission/authority) ■ The German armed forces were reduced to an army of 100,000, a small navy (only 6 battleships), no tanks or war planes ■ **Rhineland** (land between France and line 50 km to east of the River Rhine) was to be a de-militarised zone (i.e. no German soldiers were allowed). Allied troops were to remain on the west bank for 15 years ■ **Anschluss** (union) with Austria forbidden ■ Germany was to accept Clause 231 – the **War Guilt Clause** ■ Germany had to pay compensation, fixed by the Reparations Committee in 1921 at £6,600 million.

- Treaty of St Germain, 1919 (Austria)

- Treaty of Trianon, 1920 (Hungary)

- Treaty of Neuilly, 1919 (Bulgaria)

- Treaties of Sèvres, 1920 and Lausanne, 1923 (Turkey)

- assessing the Treaties (problems: especially Germany, Hungary, Czechoslovakia and Poland; fairness)

- the establishment of the League of Nations

This section deals with the problems of peace-making with Germany focusing on:

■ the "Big Three" and their aims

■ the Treaty of Versailles

This section tests your skills in comparing or cross-referencing different sources. For this type of question you need to refer in detail to the sources to show how they agree *and* how they disagree about a particular historical event.

FactZONE

You need to learn these key facts about the "Big Three" and their aims:

1914–1918 Britain and France built up tremendous debts to finance the First World War. Large areas of the north of France were devastated.

"The Big Three" David Lloyd George (British PM), Georges "Tiger" Clemenceau (French PM), and Woodrow Wilson (US President).

Britain

(wanted **compromise peace**)

750,000 killed and 1.5 million casualties.

The war cost £10 billion (£1 billion borrowed from the USA).

The British people wanted harsh peace and compensation.

Lloyd George feared a harsh treaty would create future bitterness and make Germany too weak to resist communism. Also he wanted to maintain Britain's empire, and to begin trading with Germany as soon as possible, to help British industry.

France

(wanted **harsh peace**)

1.4 million killed and 2.5 million casualties. There was massive destruction of land, factories (25,000), railway lines (5,600 km) and roads (48,000 km).

The French people wanted Germany to pay **reparations** (compensation) of 200,000 million gold francs to cover damage and war debts.

Clemenceau wanted Germany to lose much of its land and industry, and to greatly reduce its armed forces, to pay France's debts, and keep Germany weak and unable to attack France again.

USA

(wanted **a just peace**)

The USA was not invaded; it suffered only small losses and had no war debts. It entered the war in 1917 as "a war to end wars".

Woodrow Wilson did not fully support Britain and France. He wanted **self-determination** (people ruling themselves) and **international cooperation** (peaceful settling of disputes).

Jan 1918 Fourteen Points were issued by Wilson as a foundation for long-term peace.

The Treaty of Versailles

28 June 1919 The Treaty of Versailles was signed without consulting the new democratic Weimar government in Germany. It was called a **Diktat** (dictated peace).

There were eight main points to the Treaty of Versailles (see previous page).

The treaty also caused certain problems. Many Germans didn't know the war was going badly for them and they felt betrayed by their own politicians who'd signed the **armistice** (cease-fire agreement) and the treaty. In Germany they became known as the **November Criminals**. There was no self-determination or **plebiscite** (referendum, i.e. a vote by the people on one particular issue) for Germans transferred to Poland, or for German-speakers in Austria and parts of Czechoslovakia.

Comparing different sources

REMEMBER Comparing a few different sources means explaining how far the sources agree or disagree about something, or differ from each other, as well as being **similar**.

📺 The "Big Three" and their aims

Here are two sources about the post-war aims of France.

Source A A French poster produced after the First World War. (Text says: Murderers always return to the scenes of their crime.)

B

In the view of the Allied Powers the war which began on August 1 1914, was the greatest crime against humanity and the freedom of peoples that any nation calling itself civilised has ever committed. Germany's responsibility is not confined to having planned and started the war. She is no less responsible for the savage and inhuman manner in which it was conducted. The conduct of Germany is almost unexampled in human history. No less than seven million dead lie buried in Europe because Germany saw fit to go to war. There must be justice for the dead. There must be justice for the people who now stagger under war debts. There must be justice for those millions whose homes and lands the German savagery has spoiled and destroyed.

Source B Extract from the Allied statement to the German representatives.

◎ *To what extent do sources A and B provide a similar view of French aims during the peace negotiations of 1919?*

REMEMBER To get high marks you must make **detailed** references to **all** the sources mentioned.

Similarities: Both sources are similar in that they point to the great death and destruction resulting from the German invasion. Source A mentions "murderers" and source B says "seven million dead", etc.

Differences: Source A shows fear while source B also tries to place blame (war guilt) on Germany, and makes reference to justice and compensation.

◎ *Now highlight any points given in the sources and/or in the provenance details, using one colour for similarities and another for differences.*

📺 The Treaty of Versailles

Study sources A and B below, which are about the Treaty of Versailles.

❗ R E M E M B E R
Try to make clear references to **both** sources.

Source A British cartoon about the Treaty of Versailles produced in 1919.

A

PEACE AND FUTURE CANNON FODDER

The Tiger: "Curious! I seem to hear a child weeping!"

B

It was a peace of vengeance. It reeked with injustice. It was incapable of fulfilment. It sowed a thousand seeds from which new wars might spring... The absurdity, the wild impossiblity, of extracting that vast tribute (reparations) from the defeated enemy... ought to have been obvious to the most ignorant schoolboy...

Source B A British journalist's view of the Treaty of Versailles, 1929.

❓ *Think about how you can show where and how the sources are similar and/or different.*

◉ *Use two different colours to highlight any similarities and differences between the sources and/or the details of their origins.*

Practice question – the peace treaties

Study sources A and B above and write one or two paragraphs to answer the question. Allow yourself 15 minutes.

■ To what extent do sources A and B agree about the terms of the Treaty of Versailles?

The League of Nations established

To be able to answer questions on this topic, you will need to know about the following:

• the **Articles of the Covenant** (rules) of the League of Nations

• the structure of the League (Council, Assembly, Secretariat, Special Commissions and Committees)

• **isolationism** (non-involvement) and non-membership of the USA

• non-membership of Germany, Austria and Russia

• Britain and France (domination of the League, differences)

• Conference of Ambassadors (Britain, France, Italy and Japan)

• powers (economic sanctions, restrictions on trade, lack of armed forces, failure of the Geneva Protocol)

• the Locarno Treaties (1925) and German membership (1926)

• administrative and economic aid

• settlement of disputes 1920-1929 (successes and failures – the importance of Britain and France, and the absence of the USA)

This section deals with the work of the League in settling disputes in the years 1920-1929, focusing on:

■ successes

■ failures

This section tests your comprehension and knowledge. For this you need to look closely at the source *and* use your own knowledge of the topic to interpret the source and add to or explain the information it contains.

You need to learn these key facts.

Successes

1920   The League stopped Yugoslavia invading Albania.

1920–1921   It settled the dispute between Finland and Sweden over the **Aaland Islands**, in Finland's favour.

1921–1922   It settled the dispute between Poland and Germany over **Upper Silesia**, in Poland's favour, after holding a **plebiscite** (referendum) on the question of the border.

1924–1925   It settled the dispute between Iraq and Turkey over the **Mosul** area (important for oil), in Iraq's favour. (Iraq was a British mandate area.)

1925   It stopped war between Bulgaria and Greece, ordering Greece to withdraw its troops and pay compensation.

Failures

1920   The League was unable to solve the dispute between Poland and Lithuania over the town of **Vilna** which was seized by Poland. Poland ignored the League's attempts to mediate and a Conference of Ambassadors later agreed to Polish control.

1920–1921   It failed to stop war between Poland and Russia. (The League members Britain and France backed Poland.)

1920–1922   It failed to stop war between Turkey and Greece (but helped with the refugee problem).

1923   The League was unable to prevent Italy's seizure of the Greek island of **Corfu** (the Corfu Incident). France, not wishing to upset Italy, blocked action by the League.

The League was also unable to prevent Lithuania seizing the German port of **Memel**. A Conference of Ambassadors also failed. (Eventually Lithuania accepted the League's suggestion of Memel as an "international zone".)

The League couldn't prevent the French and Belgian invasion of the **Ruhr** because of Germany's non-payment of the second instalment of reparations. France didn't even consult the League.

☷ Successes of the League 1920–1929

Study the source below, which is a British cartoon about the formation and membership of the League of Nations, published in a British magazine.

THE GAP IN THE BRIDGE.

❗ REMEMBER
For this type of question you need to extract as much information as possible from the source (dates, references to events, laws, individuals, etc.).

Then use your own knowledge of the topic to help explain what is in the source.

◎ *Using this source, and your own knowledge, explain what the cartoon seems to suggest about the ability of the League of Nations to settle disputes in its early years.*

The source shows that the USA did not join, even though the League was Woodrow Wilson's idea. The cartoon suggests that without the USA the League would not be successful. It is correct to say that in the absence of the USA, the most important members of the League were France and Britain.

From your own knowledge you will know that despite the absence of the USA, the League *was* successful to some extent, but only in solving disputes involving less powerful countries.

📺 Failures of the League 1920–1929

Study the source below, which is a British cartoon from the *London Standard* about the Corfu Incident in 1923. The smiling figure in the middle is Mussolini.

Mussolini   Poincaré   Cecil

THE NEW MEMBER

◎ *Highlight the information given by the source, and/or by the details of its origin.*

⁇ *What is happening, who/what is shown, and what kind of impression does the source seem to give?*

⁇ *Use your own knowledge to give a fuller explanation. You will need to consider other failures during the period 1920-1929.*

Practice question – failures of the League

Use the source above *and* your own knowledge to answer the following question. Allow yourself 20 minutes.

■ Explain what this source tells us about the League's inability to settle disputes involving more powerful nations.

To be able to answer questions on this topic, you will need to know about the following:

• the impact of the Great Depression (unemployment, political extremism/fascism)

• aggressive nationalist foreign policies (Italy, Germany, Japan)

• 1931-1932: the Japanese invasion of Manchuria (the Lytton Commission, and the League's criticism of Japan)

• 1932-1934: the League's failure to prevent war between Bolivia and Paraguay, although it settled a dispute between Columbia and Peru. The Soviet Union joined the League, but Japan and Germany left

• 1935: Italy's invasion of Abyssinia/Ethiopia (limited economic sanctions, failure of the Hoare-Laval Pact)

• 1936: the League's failure to act over Nazi Germany's re-occupation of the Rhineland. The League's failure to take effective action against German and Italian involvement in the Spanish Civil War

• 1937: Japan invaded China. Italy left the League in December

• 1938-39: Germany's invasion of Austria (Anschluss) and Czechoslovakia. Italy's invasion of Albania

This section deals with the increasing ineffectiveness of the League in the 1930s, focusing on:

■ Manchuria

■ Abyssinia (now called Ethiopia)

This section tests your ability to evaluate sources for usefulness. For questions like this, you need to focus on what information the source actually provides about a particular historical event, *and* use your own knowledge about that event. The usefulness of the source depends on what questions are being asked as well as what the sources have to offer. The origin of the source is important in deciding on the accuracy of the information. Was it produced by someone who knew the truth? Was it produced by someone who was biased and likely to give unreliable information?

Manchuria

1926   Hirohito became emperor of Japan.

1930–1931   Japan's industry, which never could produce enough of its own raw materials (e.g. coal, iron, oil), was hit hard by the Great Depression, and peasant farmers were ruined by the drop in prices of agricultural produce. The emperor, army generals and **zaibatsu** (large industrial companies) decided on the expansion of the Japanese empire (Korea had been a colony since 1905) as a solution to its economic problems.

Sept 1931   The Mukden Incident took place: the Japanese troops in Kwantung area staged an explosion on part of the Japanese-owned South Manchurian Railway. Japan blamed the Chinese troops, and then occupied part of Manchuria (part of China, which was also a member of the League). The civilian government was increasingly unable to control the army and zaibatsu.

Oct 1931   China appealed to the League of Nations, and the Japanese government ordered its army to withdraw, but the army continued to advance into Manchuria.

Dec 1931   The Japanese troops occupied all of Manchuria. The League didn't impose sanctions on Japan, but instead sent a Commission of Enquiry to investigate the facts.

Feb 1932   Japan said Manchuria was now an independent state (Manchukuo) and installed Puyi (the last emperor of China) as a "puppet" ruler.

Nov 1932   The Commission of Enquiry's report (the Lytton Report) condemned Japan.

Feb 1933   The League accepted the Report and ordered Japan to withdraw from Manchuria/Manchukuo. Japan left the League.

Abyssinia

1922   Mussolini's Fascist Party took over in Italy.

1930–1933   The economic problems in Italy were made worse by the Great Depression. Mussolini wanted war and a bigger empire to solve his political and economic problems.

1934   Italian troops provoked clashes with Abyssinian troops on the borders of the Italian colony, Somaliland. The League investigated this.

Oct 1935   The Italian army invaded Abyssinia (a member of the League) and used poison gas, bombs and tanks. The Emperor Haile Selassie appealed to the League for help.

Nov 1935   Britain and France did not close the Suez Canal to Italian supply ships. (Italy was seen as a useful ally against Nazi Germany - Mussolini had signed the "Stresa Front"). The League imposed only limited economic sanctions, although Italy was accused of aggression.

Dec 1935   Britain and France proposed the Hoare-Laval Pact which would have allowed Italy to have two-thirds of Abyssinia. But public opinion forced the plan to be dropped.

March 1936   Britain and France finally imposed sanctions on oil and petrol - but too late.

May 1936   The Italian army captured Addis Ababa, the capital of Abyssinia. Later, they conquered the whole of Abyssinia and renamed it Ethiopia.

July 1936   The League ended all sanctions against Italy.

Dec 1937   Italy left the League.

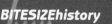

📺 Manchuria

Study the two sources below, which are about the crisis over Manchuria.

Source A A British cartoon about the League of Nations' policy on the Japanese invasion of Manchuria, 1931

Source B A comment about the Manchurian crisis from a British newspaper.

> ! **REMEMBER**
> When you comment on the usefulness of sources, discuss in detail all the sources mentioned; their origin; whether they are primary or secondary; and how accurate the information is (using your own knowledge).

> B
>
> The League Covenant [the charter of the League setting out its principles] can apparently be ignored with impunity. Japan has ignored it by invading Manchuria; the nations represented on the League Council have ignored it by refusing to insist on the withdrawal of Japanese troops. The Covenant has failed to save China from aggression as completely as a signed and ratified treaty failed to save Belgium from German aggression in 1914. The Great Powers, despite all their fine gestures, have to their great shame not even seriously prostested against, let alone resisted, such a state of affairs.

> ! **REMEMBER**
> Even biased or unreliable sources can be useful, e.g. as historical evidence of propaganda or how particular people/organisations thought/felt about an issue.

◎ *How useful are these sources as historical evidence of how the League of Nations dealt with the crisis in Manchuria?*

Source A is a primary source. It makes useful references to the Lytton Report, the lack of a strong response from the League, and Japan's armed defiance of the League. But it doesn't provide detailed information. Also the cartoonist is British and clearly critical of the League so he may have exaggerated.

Source B is also a primary source. It is useful because it refers to the Japanese invasion and the League's order to withdraw. But it is from a British newspaper. This source too is critical of the League and doesn't give the Japanese point of view.

Both sources agree on the lack of effective action.

⊙ Abyssinia

Study the two sources below, which are about the crisis over Abyssinia.

Source A A British cartoon about the League of Nations' policy over Abyssinia.

THE AWFUL WARNING.

FRANCE AND ENGLAND
(together?).
"WE DON'T WANT YOU TO FIGHT,
BUT, BY JINGO, IF YOU DO,
WE SHALL PROBABLY ISSUE A JOINT MEMORANDUM
SUGGESTING A MILD DISAPPROVAL OF YOU."

B

I claim that justice which is due to my people and the assistance promised it eight months ago. That assistance has been constantly refused me. I assert the problem submitted to the Assembly today is a much wider one than that of the situation created by Italy's aggression... It is the very existence of the League of Nations that is at stake.

Source B Extract from the speech by Haile Selassie (Emperor of Abyssinia) to the League of Nations, 1936.

⊙ *Highlight any information given by the sources, and/or by the provenance details.*

② *Think about whether one source is likely to be more or less biased than the other, how the sources agree or differ, and the positive and negative features of each source.*

❗ **REMEMBER** Comment on the origin, the nature, and the purpose of the source.

Practice question – Abyssinia

Study sources A and B and write two or three paragraphs to answer the following question. Allow yourself 15 minutes.

■ How useful are these sources for showing how the League of Nations responded to the Italian invasion of Abyssinia in 1935?

Lenin and Revolution 1917–1924

To be able to answer questions on this topic, you will need to know about the following:

- the problems of Tsarist Russia (land, industry, society)

- the political opposition before 1914 (Liberals, Social Revolutionaries, Marxists)

- the impact of the First World War on Russia (casualties at the front, food shortages at home)

- the Revolution of March 1917

- problems of the Provisional Government (land, war)

- the growth of the Bolsheviks (Lenin's return, April Theses, July Days, Kornilov's attempted coup)

- the Bolshevik Revolution, November 1917

- Treaty of Brest-Litovsk, and Civil War:
Trotsky, **Commissar** (minister) for War, forms the **Red** (pro-Bolshevik) Army. It began as a volunteer army, based on the Red Guards. By 1919, the Red Army faced four White armies, led by Kolchak, Denikin, Yudenich and Wrangel. By 1921, using ex-Tsarist officers and conscription, the Red Army numbered five million.

- War Communism and the New Economic Policy (NEP)

- Lenin's Testament and death

This section deals with the Bolsheviks in power 1917-1924 focusing on:

- the Civil War, 1918-1920
- economic policies, 1917 -1924

This section tests your skills of comparing sources.

You need to learn these key facts:

Civil War, 1918–1920

March 1918   **Treaty of Brest-Litovsk:** ended Russia's part in the First World War but resulted in Russia losing to Germany 74% of iron and coal mines, 27% of farm land, 26% of railways, and 26% of population (due to change of nationality). The Treaty also angered the Social Revolutionaries, who quit the coalition government with the Bolsheviks.

May 1918   **Czech Legion:** 45,000 prisoners of war seized the Trans-Siberian Railway and towns along it. Enemies of the Bolsheviks used the opportunity to form **White** (anti-Bolshevik) armies, and to march on Moscow. This was the beginning of the Civil War.

Dec. 1918   **Foreign intervention:** Troops from Britain, France, USA, Japan, Poland and Finland were sent to help the Whites. This turned many peasants against the Whites.

1919–1920   War on several fronts. By early 1920, the Reds controlled the central areas and were winning the upper hand. Foreign troops began to withdraw. The Reds had won the Civil War.

Economic Policies, 1917–1924

1918   War Communism was introduced as emergency measures for food and industry during the Civil War. ■ Banks and most factories were nationalised (i.e. government took over). ■ Discipline was enforced in factories. ■ Private trade was banned. Peasants were forced to sell surplus food to government at fixed prices. ■ Rationing of food was introduced in cities. ■ Money was allowed to lose value – **barter** (exchange of foods) was encouraged.

By 1919, peasants planted less corn, hid surplus, kept fewer animals. Despite requisition squads, a serious food shortage in 1920 became, in 1921, a famine in parts of Russia.
Lenin failed to persuade the rest of the Bolshevik government to change economic policy.

March 1921   Kronstadt Rising – 10,000 sailors at this naval base began the most serious of several protests against War Communism. New Economic Policy (NEP) replaced War Communism. This meant that:
■ Fixed amount of corn was paid by peasants as tax.
■ Peasants were allowed to sell surplus food for a profit.
■ Less tax for peasants who increased production.
■ Some smaller factories were returned to owners or leased out.
■ Money was used again, and private trading was allowed.

The Red Army crushed the revolt, but many Bolsheviks now began to listen to Lenin's new plans. Though many communists saw NEP as a step back to capitalism, it proved effective. By 1925 food production figures were back to 1913 levels and industrial production was also up considerably. Some people became rich:
■ **nepmen** (private traders)
■ **kulaks** (rich peasants)

Russia in Revolution 1917–1941

REMEMBER When comparing sources you need to explain to what extent the sources agree and/or disagree about something, making detailed references to **all** the sources mentioned.

34

Civil War

Here are two sources about the Civil War.

Source A Cartoon of three White generals produced by the Bolsheviks in 1919. The dogs are named Denikin, Kolchak and Yudenich.

Source B Map of the Civil War in Russia.

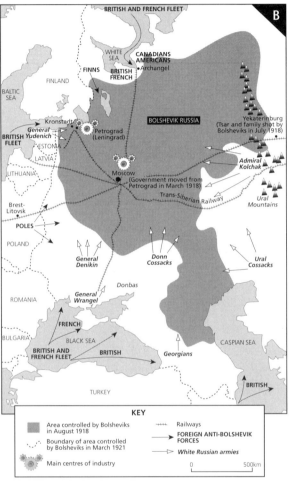

REMEMBER To gain high marks, you must show how all the sources contain **similar** information; and show how the sources **differ**. For example one source may contain extra information, or one may not be as reliable as another.

◎ *To what extent do sources A and B provide a similar impression of the White forces in the Civil War in Russia?*

Similarities: Sources A and B both give the names of the White generals. Both sources make references to the foreign countries involved.

Differences: Source B only shows foreign involvement. Source A, which is a Bolshevik propaganda poster from the Civil War (therefore likely to be biased), goes further and implies that the White generals were merely the puppets of the foreign powers.

◎ *Highlight any points in the sources, using one colour for similarities and another for differences.*

Economic policies

Study sources A and B below, which are about the New Economic Policy.

Source A

Table of production figures, Russia, 1913–1926							A
	1913	**1921**	**1922**	**1923**	**1925**	**1926**	
Grain (million tonnes)	80	37	50	57	73	77	
Cattle (millions)	59		46		62		
Pigs (millions)	20		12		22		
Coal (million tonnes)	29	9	10	14	18	27	
Steel (million tonnes)	4	0.2	0.7	0.7	2	3	

Source B Extract from a Bolshevik's memoirs of 1992, about the introduction of the NEP.

> There wasn't a scrap of food in the country. We were down to our last small piece of bread per person, then suddenly they announced the NEP. Cafés started opening, restaurants, factories went back into private hands; it was capitalism. The papers kept quoting Lenin - 'Two steps forward, one step back'; that's all very well but in my eyes what was happening was what I'd struggled against. I can remember the years 1921 and 1922; we used to discuss NEP for hours on end at party meetings. Most people supported Lenin, others said he was wrong; many tore up their party cards.

B

Russia in Revolution 1917–1941

⊚ *Highlight any points in the sources, or in the provenance details provided, using one colour for similarities and another for differences.*

⍰ *Think about how the sources are similar and at what points. Then think about where and how they differ.*

Practice question – economic policies

Study sources A and B above and write two or three paragraphs to answer the question. Allow yourself 20 minutes.

■ To what extent do sources A and B agree that the New Economic Policy was a success?

To be able to answer questions on this topic, you will need to know about the following:

- Stalin's early career, before 1917

- Stalin's rise, 1917-1924, to **Commissar** (Minister) for Nationalities and General Secretary of Communist Party

- the struggle for power (Trotsky and the Left, Bukharin and the Right).

- collectivisation of agriculture (i.e. joining small private farms into larger state farms), struggle against the kulaks (rich peasants), and its effects

- industrialisation and the Five Year Plans (heavy industry and the First Five Year Plan; Stakhanovite workers; light industry and the Second and Third Five Year Plans; effects).

- purges and Show Trials (murder of Kirov, elimination of "Old Bolsheviks", purge of the armed forces' officers)

- Soviet foreign policy (failure to form alliance with Britain and France against Nazi Germany, Nazi-Soviet Non-Aggression Pact)

- the Great Fatherland War (Operation Barbarossa, "scorched earth" policy, battles of Leningrad and Stalingrad)

This section deals with Stalin's policies to transform the Soviet economy 1928-1941, focusing on:

■ collectivisation of agriculture

■ industrialisation and the Five Year Plans

This section tests your ability to evaluate sources for usefulness. For questions like this, you need to focus on what information the source actually provides about a particular historical event, and use your own knowledge about that event. The usefulness of the source depends on what questions are being asked as well as what the sources have to offer. The origin of the source is important in deciding on the accuracy of the information. Was it produced by someone who knew the truth? Was it produced by someone who was biased and likely to give unreliable information?

Stalin's Second Revolution – his aims and methods

1924–1928   Stalin continued Lenin's NEP (New Economic Policy); the peasants retained private ownership of their land and were allowed to sell food for profit. The pace of industrialisation was slow. Stalin opposed the Left Opposition's calls for change.

1928–1941   Stalin was concerned at Russia's economic backwardness in agriculture and industry. He feared an attack by capitalist countries (particularly Germany after 1933), so he decided to **modernise** rapidly.

Collectivisation: Industrialisation needed more factory workers and fewer, more efficient peasants, but by 1928, agriculture was producing two million tonnes *less* grain than was needed. Stalin decided that 25 million individual peasant holdings should be joined into 250,000 state collective farms (**kolkhozes**). Peasants were to pool equipment, animals and land in each kolkhoz. Machine Tractor Stations were set up to provide tractors and repair the machinery. Collectivisation began in 1929.

Results: In 1930, many better-off peasants (**kulaks**) slaughtered their animals rather than hand them over. Stalin therefore decided to destroy the kulaks as a class: 1.5 million out of 5 million kulaks were deported to poorer parts of USSR. Many who resisted were executed. By 1935, 85% of all land had been collectivised. But the destruction and chaos of collectivisation led to a drop in food production and famine in parts of the USSR during 1932-33. Food production levels did not return to the 1928 figures until 1939.

Industrialisation and the Five Year Plans

1928–1932   *First Five Year Plan* This was drawn up by **Gosplan** which was the State Planning Commission. The plan concentrated on *heavy industry* (iron, steel, coal, electricity, oil, machinery). These industries were given high targets for increased production.

1933–1937   *Second Five Year Plan* This plan continued the emphasis on *heavy industry* – especially tractors for collective farms. To encourage workers to work harder, bonus payments were made to those who exceeded the targets (norms). "Shock-brigades" of super-workers were used as propaganda to motivate others. They were called **Stakhanovites**, after Stakhanov, a miner who'd produced a record amount of coal in one day in 1935.

1938–1941   *Third Five-Year Plan* This plan concentrated on *light industry*, to produce more consumer goods. It was quite successful, but was abandoned in 1940 because of fear of invasion. Instead, the emphasis shifted to armaments.

Results: Despite problems, production did greatly increase (though most targets were too high to be met) and many new canals, railways, dams and industrial centres were built.

Overall Assessment

Positive: By 1941, despite problems, collectivisation and the Five Year Plans had turned the Soviet Union into a major industrial country. Some historians claim that without this, the USSR would never have defeated Nazi Germany and that Hitler might have won the Second World War.

Negative: There was much wastage and suffering. The problems caused by collectivisation weakened the USSR and for the first years of the Five Year Plans, living conditions didn't improve.

📺 Collectivisation

Here are two sources about collectivisation.

38

❗ REMEMBER Whenever you comment on the usefulness of sources, discuss: all the sources mentioned in detail; their origin; whether they are primary or secondary sources; how accurate the information is (using your own knowledge).

Source A Photograph of Soviet peasants, 1923.

> A radical change is taking place in the development of our agriculture from small, backward, individual farming. We are advancing full steam ahead along the path of industrialisation to Socialism, leaving behind the age-long 'Russian' backwardness. We are becoming a country of metal, a country of cars, a country of tractors, and when we have put the USSR in a car, and a peasant on a tractor, let the capitalists try to overtake us.

Source B Extract from Stalin's explanation of the new policy of collectivisation, 1929.

❗ REMEMBER Even biased or unreliable sources can be useful, e.g. as historical evidence of propaganda or of how particular people/organisations thought/felt about an issue.

◎ *How useful are these sources for showing why collectivisation of agriculture was introduced by Stalin in 1929?*

Source A is a primary source, although it shows conditions in 1923 rather than 1929 and therefore things might have improved by then. It is useful for showing the backwardness of agriculture.

Source B is also primary. It is just after the introduction of collectivisation; Stalin was in a position to know the reasons as he was responsible for introducing collectivisation. But the source might be biased (Stalin might have been trying to justify the policy or hide any negative aspects).

◎ *Highlight any points of information provided by the sources or by the origin details.*

Industrialisation and the Five Year Plans

Study sources A and B below, which are about the success and achievements of the Five Year Plans.

Source A A Soviet cartoon of 1933, showing a foreign capitalist's anger at the achievements of the First Five Year Plan.

Source B
Table of industrial output, 1927-1940. Compiled from Soviet and Western sources by an economic historian.

B	1927	1930	1932	1935	1937	1940
Coal (million tonnes)	36	61	65	102	130	152
Steel (million tonnes)	3	5	6	13	18	18
Oil (million tonnes)	12	17	21	24	26	26
Electricity (million kWh)	18	22	20	45	80	90

⊚ *Highlight any useful information provided by the sources, or by the details of their origin.*

(?) *Think about whether one source is likely to be more or less biased than the other.*

(?) *Consider whether the information or viewpoint of the sources agree. Can you find the positive and negative features of both sources?*

❗ **REMEMBER** When answering this kind of question, comment on the origin of both sources.

Practice question – the Five Year Plans

Write two or three paragraphs. Allow yourself 20 minutes.

■ How useful are these sources as information about the success of the first three Five Year Plans?

Weimar Germany 1919–1933

To be able to answer questions on this topic, you will need to know about the following:

- the end of the First World War

- German Revolution (abdication of the Kaiser, the role of Ebert and the SPD (Social Democrats), the Spartacists)

- Weimar Republic and its constitution

- the Treaty of Versailles (dictated peace or **Diktat,** War Guilt clause, the "November criminals")

- opposition to the Weimar Republic – Kapp's **Putsch,** (armed revolt); Red Rising in the Ruhr

- hyper-inflation of 1923 (French invasion of the Ruhr, the Beer Hall Putsch)

- the Stresemann Years, 1924-1929

- impact of the Great Depression (mass unemployment, rise of Nazis)

- collapse of Weimar (coalition governments, rule by Presidential decree, 1932 elections)

This section deals with Weimar Germany 1919-1929, before the Great Depression, focusing on:

■ the Weimar Constitution

■ hyper-inflation of 1923

This section tests your skills of comprehension, i.e. understanding historical sources and what they are telling you.

You need to learn these key facts:

The Weimar Constitution

Feb 1919   Ebert, a Social Democrat, was elected President of the new German republic.

Aug 1919   The Constitution of the new republic was drawn up in Weimar and accepted.

The New Constitution

The new constitution was Germany's first experience of a real democracy. Before 1919, the **Kaiser** (emperor) controlled the government, foreign affairs and the armed forces.
Weimar set up a new **Reichstag** (parliament) elected by everybody over twenty in a secret ballot, every four years.
Seats in the Reichstag were awarded by proportional representation (PR), so that if a party won 35% of the votes for example, it got 35% of the seats.
The constitution included *Fundamental Rights* (individual citizens' rights).
Weimar set up a *federal system* where power was shared between the central government in Berlin and 18 new **Länder** (state) governments.
A president was elected separately for seven years, to act as a check on the Reichstag's power.

Potential Problems

Germany was not used to democracy, as democracy under the Kaiser had been very limited.
Although the Kaiser had fled, the senior civil servants, judges, police chiefs and army officers who had supported him kept their jobs.
Article 48 of the Constitution allowed the President to announce a "state of emergency", and bypass the Reichstag by ruling by decree.
In the four difficult years 1919-1923, Germany had nine coalition governments.

Hyper-inflation, 1923

1921   Versailles Reparations Committee fixed Germany's payment at £6,600 million over 66 years. The first instalment was paid in gold, coal, iron, and wood.

1922   The German government said it was unable to pay the second instalment because the economy was too weak after the war, and the printing of extra banknotes was causing inflation.

1923   French and Belgian troops entered the Ruhr to take goods from Germany in place of the second instalment of reparations. The German workers went on strike and refused to cooperate with the invaders. The German government paid the strikers for passive resistance by printing even more banknotes. Inflation increased rapidly during January to November 1923, so much so that it was called **hyper-inflation**. Workers were paid twice a *day* because money devalued so quickly. There was much hunger and suffering, especially for those on fixed incomes (pensioners) or with savings. In September, Gustav Stresemann headed a new government and in November introduced the new currency called the Rentenmark to end inflation. The Nazis' attempted **putsch** failed.

The Weimar Constitution

Here is a source showing the results of the elections in Germany 1919-1928.

| | % of votes won | | | | |
	1919	1920	1924		1928
			May	Dec	
German Communist Party (KPD)	-	2	12	9	11
Social Democratic Party (SPD)	38	21	21	26	30
German Democratic Party (DDP)	19	8	6	6	5
Centre Party	20	18	17	18	15
German People's Party (DVP)	4	14	9	10	9
German Nationalist Party (DNVP)	10	15	19	21	14
Nazi Party (NSDAP)	-	-	7	3	2
Other (minor) parties	9	22	9	7	14

! REMEMBER Comprehension questions ask you to show that you understand the information in a source. Sometimes you will need to point out two or three separate pieces of information.

◎ *According to this source which three parties tended to dominate the elections of this period?*

What do these election results tell us about politics in Weimar Germany?

According to the source, the SPD, Centre Party, and the DNVP dominated the elections.

! REMEMBER To get high marks, it is not enough to list the main individual points - you must also make your own overall summary of what the source is saying. Don't just copy bits from the sources.

Proportional representation meant it was difficult for one party to have an outright majority. Consequently there were frequent coalition governments. Constant changes made it difficult to deal with the serious political and economic problems during the period 1919-1923.

◎ *Highlight the three dominant parties and their percentage of the vote in the source.*

The hyper-inflation of 1923

Study the source below, which is a comment about the hyper-inflation in Germany in 1923, written many years after the events described.

! REMEMBER
Identify the main problems separately. Write a summary at the beginning or the end.

> As soon as factory gates opened and the workers streamed out, pay packets (often in old cigar boxes) in their hands, their wives grabbed the money and rushed to the nearest shops to buy food before the prices went up again. Salaries always lagged behind. People living on fixed incomes sank into deeper and deeper poverty.
>
> A familiar sight in the streets was of people carrying laundry baskets full of paper money. It sometimes happened that thieves stole the baskets, but tipped out the money and left it on the spot.

◎ *Highlight the problems mentioned by the source.*

⸮ *Consider how you can use your own knowledge of the hyper-inflation to add to the information given in the source and explain why it happened.*

Practice questions – the hyper-inflation of 1923

Use the source above to answer the following questions. Allow yourself 20 minutes.

■ According to the source above, what were the main problems caused by the hyper-inflation?

■ Why did hyper-inflation occur in 1923?

Germany 1919–1945

The rise of the Nazis 1920–1933

To be able to answer questions on this topic, you will need to know about the following:

- Hitler and the origins of the Nazi Party

- the Munich Beer Hall Putsch, 1923 (including Hitler's trial and imprisonment)

- Nazi beliefs (*Mein Kampf*)

- the Nazi Party in the 1920s (The "Lean" Years, or Years of Waiting, party reorganisation)

- the impact of the Great Depression (mass unemployment, political extremism)

- the Nazis' rise to power (breakdown of the Weimar constitution, elections 1930-1932, political deals)

This section deals with the Nazi Party in the years 1920-1933, focusing on:

■ party developments in the 1920s

■ how Hitler became **Chancellor** (the equivalent of prime minister) in 1933.

This section gives you practice at answering causation essay questions. For these questions you need to explain *why* things happened.

To get yourself started, try to write down 5 or 6 separate points which relate to the topic – these can then become the basis for a series of paragraphs.

To get high marks, make a plan and sort the explanations and causes into order according to which was more or less important, or according to time (long, medium, or short term causes) so that you don't just list the facts.

Finally, try to write a concluding paragraph which includes a judgement about the cause(s) you think was/were the most important.

You need to learn these key facts:

The Nazi Party in the 1920s

1923   The Munich Putsch (also known as Beer Hall Putsch or the National Revolution) to overthrow the government in Berlin failed.

1924   Trial and imprisonment of Hitler for high treason. Hitler wrote **Mein Kampf** (*My Struggle*) in Landsberg prison. He was released after serving nine months of a five-year sentence. The Nazis did badly in the December 1924 elections (won 14 seats).

1925   The Nazi Party was refounded after it had split and been banned. The SA (**Sturmabteilung** – Stormtroopers), which had been set up in 1921, adopted the brown shirt as uniform, and the swastika became the official party emblem.
The SS (**Schutzstaffeln** – protection squads) were set up with the black shirt as their uniform. More radical policies were abandoned, e.g. the confiscation of firms was altered to apply only to Jews.

1926   Special organisations were set up to recruit students, teachers, and young people.

1927   The party organisation was centralised under Hitler's control.

1928   Membership rose to 100,000, but there was another poor performance in the 1928 elections (12 seats). The German economy experienced a fourth consecutive good year.

Hitler comes to power

1929   In the USA the stock market crashed (Wall Street Crash), bringing an end to loans to Germany (Dawes Plan, Young Plan).

1930–1932   Germany saw a rapid increase in unemployment – over 5 million by 1932. Goebbels improved Nazi propaganda and organised mass rallies across Germany. Nazis began to get financial support from companies.
Hitler got 13 million votes compared to Hindenburg's 19 million in the 1932 Presidential election. Democracy failed in that there was a succession of weak minority coalition governments (Bruning, Van Papen) ruling by decree.
The Nazi Party greatly increased its vote and by July 1932, it was the largest single party in the Reichstag (230 seats).

Nov 1932   The Nazis again won more seats (196) than any other party in election, but 34 *fewer* than in July 1932, while the Communist Party was still increasing its share (100 seats).

Dec 1932   Von Schleicher became Chancellor. He upset big business by proposing compromises with the trade unions. Von Papen proposed a deal with Hitler as Chancellor of a mainly conservative government.

Jan 1933   Hindenburg was finally persuaded to appoint Hitler as Chancellor.

Germany 1919–1945

Causation essays

📺 The Nazi Party in the 1920s

Read the source below, which is an extract from a letter by Hitler written in 1923 while he was still in prison in Landsberg Castle.

REMEMBER For causation essays, make a plan. Don't just describe what happened, explain **why** it happened. Then summarise in an opening or concluding paragraph.

> *When I resume active work it will be necessary to pursue a new policy. Instead of working to achieve power by an armed coup, we will have to hold our noses and enter the Reichstag against the Catholic and Marxist members. If outvoting them takes longer than outshooting them, at least the result will be guaranteed by their own constitution. Any lawful process is slow. Sooner or later we will have a majority, and after that – Germany!*

◉ *Why did Hitler alter the Nazi Party's organisation and political strategy in the years 1924 to 1929?*

To answer this question, you need to look at Germany's economic situation under Stresemann as well as Nazi Party developments.

This era covers only a short period, so in this case a time-scale won't be very helpful. Instead, focus should be on the relative importance of the various factors, including paragraphs on:

REMEMBER Identify several different causes or factors. Show which you think are more important and which are less important.

- failure of the Munich Putsch (1923) and splits in the Nazi Party

- success of Stresemann (Dawes Plan, 1924) in overcoming economic problems (especially unemployment)

- the need to attract political and financial support from wealthy classes

- the prosperity of 1924–1928 meant extremist actions were unpopular or unnecessary.

◉ *Highlight the information in the tips above in two colours according to general factors and factors related to the Nazi Party itself.*

⊚ Hitler comes to power

Look at the source below, which shows the results of the elections to the Reichstag, 1928-1932.

Table of number of seats won by parties in elections in Germany, 1928-1932	1928	1930	1932 July	1932 Nov
Nazis	12	107	230	196
German Nationalist Party (DNVP)	73	41	37	52
German People's Party (DVP)	45	30	7	11
Centre Party	62	68	75	70
German Democratic Party (DDP)	25	20	4	2
Social Democratic Party (SPD)	153	143	133	121
Communists	54	77	89	100
Other	67	91	33	32
Total	491	577	608	584

❗ REMEMBER First work out a rough plan. **Don't** simply write down all you know about this topic. Focus on explaining **why** (not the details of **how**) Hitler was able to become Chancellor.

(?) *Think about how you can sort the causes into long/medium/short term causes. Consider events after 1928 closely, but include relevant points about the years 1923-1928.*

(?) *Think how you can write a paragraph to sum up which cause(s), in your opinion, was/were the most important. This should help you to avoid writing an essay which simply describes what happened.*

◎ *Make sure you look carefully at your textbook and your notes before writing your answer.*

Germany 1919-1945

Practice question – Hitler comes to power

Write five or six paragraphs to answer the question below, making reference to the source above. Allow yourself 30 minutes.

■ Why was Hitler able to become Chancellor on 30 January 1933?

To be able to answer questions on this topic, you will need to know about the following:

• the Nazis' destruction of the Weimar democracy – Reichstag Fire, takeover of **Länder** (German states), the Enabling Act, the banning of other parties

• Night of the Long Knives – purge of SA; Hitler becomes the **Führer** (leader)

• establishment of a Nazi Police State (**Gestapo** – Secret State Police, concentration camps)

• economic policies (National Labour Service, public works, rearmament and conscription)

• Jewish persecution (Nuremberg Laws, Kristallnacht, Final Solution)

• young people in Nazi Germany (Hitler Youth)

• women and the 3 Ks (Children, Cooking and Church)

• Nazi propaganda

• resistance to the Nazis (youth groups e.g. Edelweiss Pirates, the Meuten, White Rose, the Swing Movement, Red Orchestre, the July Plot)

This section focuses on two aspects of Nazi Germany 1933-1945:

■ Nazi persecution of Jews

■ Nazi policies for young people

This section tests your ability to answer descriptive (or narrative) essay questions. This type of question asks you to describe certain events or policies. You should find them more straightforward than causation essays, as long as you have revised widely enough.

FactZONE

You need to learn these key facts:

Nazi persecution of Jews, 1933–1945

March 1933   The Nazis set up the Department of Racial Hygiene.

April 1933   The SA were ordered to organise a national boycott of Jewish shops. Jews were sacked from important jobs (civil service, the law, universities and schools, newspapers, radio and film).

1934   All Jewish shops were marked with a yellow star or the word **Juden** (Jews). Separate seats were designated for Jews on buses, trains and in parks. Jewish children began to be victimised in schools.

1935   The Nuremberg Laws came into effect: Jews were no longer German citizens. This meant they had no rights and were not allowed to marry **Aryans** (non-Jews). Jews were "encouraged" to leave Germany.

1938   After a Nazi official was shot by a Jew, there followed mass destruction by the SA of shops and synagogues in which about 1000 Jews were killed and many more arrested. This incident is known as **Kristallnacht** (Crystal Night or Night of Broken Glass). Jewish businesses were taken over.

1942   The Wannsee Conference took place at which the leading Nazis decided on the "Final Solution to the Jewish Problem" and persecution turned into the Holocaust (1942-1945).

Nazi policies for young people

All youth organisations were taken over. Young people were encouraged to join the Hitler-Jugend (Hitler Youth Movement, set up in 1925). This organisation was divided into five different groups as shown in the table below.

Age	Boys	Girls
6-10	Pimpfen (Little Fellows)	-
10-14	Jungvolk (Youth Folk)	Jungmadel (Young Girls)
14-18	Hitler-Jugend (Hitler Youth)	Deutscher Madel (German Girls)

Towards the end of the 1930s, membership became compulsory (although recent evidence suggests that not all children joined).

All members attended Hitler Youth camps every year. There were special schools for Hitler Youths who got the best marks: Adolf Hitler Schools and Order Castles.

The Nazis changed the national curriculum in schools in order to stress the achievements of Hitler and the Nazis and to blame any problems on the Jews, Communists and the Weimar Republic. Teachers who disagreed were sacked.

Germany 1919–1945

Descriptive essays

Nazi persecution of the Jews 1933–1945

Look at the source below which shows a Nazi boycott of a Jewish shop.

SA and SS men enforcing a boycott of Jewish shops, 1933.

! REMEMBER Be careful to answer exactly what the question asks – don't write about a similar, related topic.

Write a rough plan first to make sure you cover all the main points.

◎ *How were Jews in Nazi Germany treated in the years 1933-1939?*

To answer this question, you need to focus on the main Nazi laws and actions. Don't describe the Final Solution and the Holocaust as it is outside the period of the question.

Include paragraphs on each of the main developments described in the Factzone on the previous page.
In the final paragraph you could point out that the Final Solution was to follow, but don't go into details.

◎ *List the main developments without looking at the Factzone. Then check back to see if you have missed anything.*

📺 Nazi policies for young people

Look at the source below, which is a photograph of a Hitler Youth Camp in Nuremberg, 1934. Then answer the question.

(?) *Work out how you can give a balanced answer to the practice question. For example, show how some young people resisted Nazi policies and propaganda. Don't just write about the policies of the Nazis.*

❗ REMEMBER
The question asks about boys and girls, so include both or you will lose half the marks. Write a rough plan first with a list of points you can then expand.

Practice question – Nazi policies for young people

Write five or six paragraphs to answer the question below, making reference to the source above. Allow yourself 30 minutes.

■ What were the lives of boys and girls like in Nazi Germany, 1933-1939?

52

To be able to answer questions on this topic, you will need to know about the following:

• the US constitution – elections of the President, Congress, (Senate and House of Representatives), the Supreme Court

• **isolationism** after the First World War (the reasons and results)

• presidents of the 1920s (Wilson, Harding, Coolidge, Hoover)

• racial and political intolerance in the 1920s (Ku Klux Klan, the Red Scare)

• prohibition and gangsters

• Republican presidents and policies 1921-1933 (big business, "laissez-faire", "rugged individualism")

• industrial boom (motor car industry, construction, consumer goods)

• the Stock Market (buying "on the margin")

• underlying problems (poverty, farming, foreign trade, speculation)

• the Wall Street Crash, October 1929

• Hoover and the Great Depression (unemployment, breadlines, "Hoovervilles")

❗ REMEMBER Always **use** any information the examiner provides about the source or its origin.

This section deals with the USA, 1921-1933, focusing on:

■ the Wall Street Crash

■ Hoover's policies during the Great Depression.

In this section you will find questions which test your understanding of the reliability of sources.

To decide how reliable sources are you need to examine the kind of source it is, who wrote it (or took the picture, etc.), its purpose, any possible bias, and whether it is a typical or unrepresentitive view.

You need to learn these key facts:

The Wall Street Crash

1921   The Immigration Act reduced the numbers of immigrants allowed into the USA. Further Immigration Acts, in 1924 and 1929, reduced the number of immigrants to 150,000 a year.

1922   The Fordney-McCumber Act put high **tariffs** (import duties) on foreign goods. This eventually led to European countries placing tariffs on American goods. US industry then found it difficult to export.

1923-1929   Coolidge, a Republican, became President. He believed in **laissez-faire** (letting businesses operate with no government controls). He said: "the business of America is business". US industry boomed, share prices rose. Many people were encouraged to buy stocks and shares **on the margin** (by paying a 10% deposit and being given credit for the rest). Many also bought consumer goods on hire purchase (**HP**). Increased prosperity led companies to over-produce. Farmers faced competition from Australia and Argentina, as well as the change from cotton to man-made materials for clothes.
Many groups in the USA did *not* share in the increased prosperity (farmers, the low-paid and Black Americans).

1929   Hoover became President. He believed in **"rugged individualism"**, i.e. that people should help themselves, without government assistance.

1929   Awareness of over-production and falling sales led to panic and the rapid selling of shares on 24th October, when 12 million shares were sold in one day, causing prices to fall. There was a complete collapse on 29th October and shareholders lost 8 billion dollars ($8,000,000,000). Banks collapsed, companies went bankrupt.

Hoover's policies, 1929-1933

1929-1930   Hoover, a Republican, believed in **laissez-faire** and **rugged individualism**. He refused to introduce unemployment benefits. He felt it was only a crisis of confidence, so at first took no action. His thinking was: "prosperity is just around the corner".

1930   The Hawley-Smoot Tariffs were introduced to increase import duties on foreign goods. Foreign countries then did the same to US goods.

1931   The Federal Farm Board bought wheat and cotton, but not enough to stop prices falling.

1932   The Reconstruction Finance Corporation was set up to lend small loans to banks, companies and farmers facing possible closure.
There was a small increase in **federal** (central) government spending on building projects, such as roads, to create new jobs. But it was too little, too late and by 1932, over 12 million people were unemployed.

The Wall Street Crash

Look at the photographic source below of an American family in the 1920s.

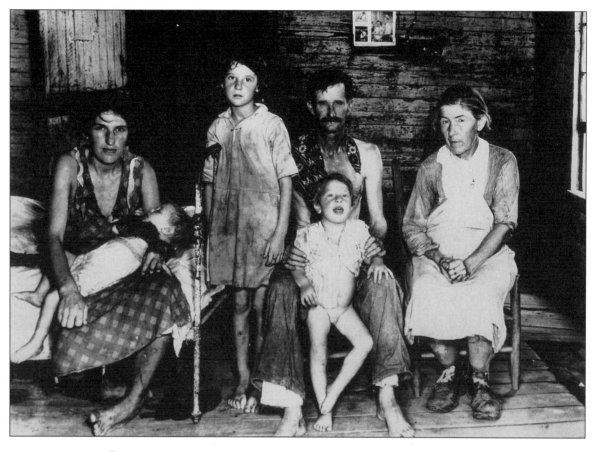

 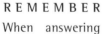 **REMEMBER** When answering reliability questions you must comment in detail on the **author,** the possible **purpose** of the source and the **nature** of the source

◎ *How reliable is this source as evidence about the prosperity of the USA in the 1920s, before the Wall Street Crash?*

This is difficult to assess as it doesn't say who took the photograph, or why. You need to raise the following points:

■ it could have been Democrat propaganda against the Republicans

■ it doesn't say when and where exactly it was taken. It could have been taken in 1929, **after** the Wall Street Crash

■ it could be an isolated example from one of the poorest states and not typical of the rest of the USA.

◎ *Highlight points provided in the source, and/or in the information about its origins.*

Hoover's policies 1929-1933

Study the source below, which shows unemployment figures in the USA during 1928-1933, compiled from official government statistics.

Year	Unemployed (millions)	Percentage of workforce
1928	2.1	4.4
1930	4.3	9
1931	8.0	16
1932	12.0	24
1933	13.0	25

(?) *When answering the practice question below, think how you can comment on:*

- *the **author** – who produced the figures?*
- ***nature** – what kind of source it is?*
- *what is its likely **purpose**?*

(?) *Think carefully about the information provided by the Chief Examiner – does it contain something you can use in your answer?*

REMEMBER
When answering questions on source reliability, think about whether the source gives an overall or only a partial view (is it **typical**?). When commenting on whether the source is primary or secondary, remember to comment on the **specific** source(s) given. Do not make general statements such as, "All photographs are biased/can be fixed," or "Primary sources are more/less reliable than secondary ones."

Practice question – Hoover's policies, 1929-1933

Use the source above to write one or two paragraphs to answer the following question. Allow yourself 15 minutes.

- How reliable is this source as evidence about the effectiveness of Hoover's policies to deal with the Great Depression?

56

To be able to answer questions on this topic, you will need to know about the following:

• the 1932 Presidential Election (Hoover, a Republican, versus Roosevelt, a Democrat)

• Roosevelt's approach: restoring confidence, government spending to get the economy going, use of federal powers (which were weak after years of Republican presidents). But not always consistent – the "Lame Duck" months (November 1932 to March 1933)

• Roosevelt's first 100 days (Emergency Banking Act, Economy Act, "fireside chats")

• the New Deal and the Alphabet Agencies

• the First New Deal, 1933-1934 (unemployed and homeless, farmers, industry)

• opposition to the New Deal (which came from conservatives, who saw Roosevelt's policies as socialist; and from radicals, who accused Roosevelt of not doing enough. The conservatives opposed the laws mainly through the Supreme Court)

• the Dust Bowl, 1934 ("Okies", "Arkies")

• Second New Deal, 1935 (Social Security Act, 1935)

• effectiveness of the New Deal (1937 Depression)

• Roosevelt's third term (1940 election, impact of the Second World War)

This section deals with the First New Deal, focusing on:

■ the New Deal laws

■ opposition to the New Deal.

This section tests your ability to answer questions which test comprehension and knowledge (comprehension in context). To answer these questions you need to look closely at the source and use your own knowledge of the topic to help you interpret the source *and* add to or explain the information it contains.

You need to learn these key facts.

First New Deal laws

The unemployed and homeless

May 1933   The Federal Emergency Relief Administration (FERA) gave 500 million dollars of food and aid to the hungry and homeless.

June 1933   The Public Works Administration (PWA) was set up to provide jobs for the unemployed with skills (schools, hospitals, dams, railways, etc.). This was part of NIRA (see below). The Home Owners Loan Corporation (HOLC) was set up.

Nov 1933   The Civil Works Administration (CWA) found jobs for four million people (but with low pay). It was disbanded in 1934.

Farmers

May 1933   The Agricultural Adjustment Administration (AAA) paid farmers to produce less and to have crops and livestock destroyed, in order to increase prices. The Farm Credit Association (FCA) provided help with mortgages and evictions.

Industry

June 1933   The National Industrial Recovery Act (NIRA) was made up of two bodies: the PWA (see above) and the National Recovery Administration (NRA). This persuaded employers to set fair wages and prices. Firms that agreed displayed the Blue Eagle sign.

Environment

April 1933   The Civilian Conservation Corps (CCC) provided work for two million unemployed single people (almost all men) in conservation work (forests, footpaths, nature reserves, etc.).

May 1933   Tennessee Valley Authority (TVA) built twenty dams to prevent floods and produce hydro-electric power.

Opposition to the New Deal

Supreme Court
The Conservatives used the Supreme Court, consisting of nine judges, to delay or destroy the New Deal laws in the following ways:
1935 The NRA was ended by the "sick chickens" case, when the Supreme Court ruled that NRA was unconstitutional as federal government had no right to interfere in state matters.
1936 The AAA was also ruled unconstitutional. In all, 11 out of 16 "alphabet agencies" were ruled against by the Supreme Court.

Radicals
1933 Huey Long, governor of Louisiana, began the "Share Our Wealth" Movement.
1935 Father Charles Coughlin, a Catholic priest, known as "the radio priest", set up the National Union for Social Justice.
1936 Frances Townsend, a retired doctor, joined with Coughlin and Gerald Smith (Long's successor) to stand against Roosevelt in the presidential elections.

The First New Deal Laws

Here is a cartoon about the New Deal, from an American newspaper, 1933.

Priming the Pump.

 REMEMBER For comprehension in context questions you must extract all possible information from the source (dates, references to events, laws, individuals, etc.) and use your own knowledge to explain what is in the source.

◉ *Using the source above, and your own knowledge, explain what the source tells us about Roosevelt's New Deal.*

The source shows Roosevelt (FDR) pouring more government money into an attempt to make emergency relief (FERA) work. The **taxpayer** is shown to have already spent **16 billion dollars**, but **7 billion dollars more** are still needed. The **leaks** show that the system is not efficient because there is wastage.

From your own knowledge you know that "priming the pump" with government money was an attempt to provide relief to the hungry and homeless and to get the economy going.
This source is an example of the criticism of the New Deal.

◉ *Highlight the relevant points from the source and/or from the details of its origin.*

Opposition to the New Deal

Study the source below, which is a cartoon showing Roosevelt riding on a merry-go-round, from the British magazine, Punch, 1937.

A British cartoon of 1937, about Roosevelt and his Second New Deal.

THE LINE OF LEAST RESISTANCE

! REMEMBER Point out all the information in the source.

? *Can you say anything about what is happening in the cartoon and what and who is shown? What kind of impression does it seem to give?*

? *What else do you know that you can add to your explanation? Think about the period 1933-1937.*

◎ *Highlight any relevant points in the source and/or in the details of its origins.*

Practice question – opposition to the New Deal

Write two or three paragraphs to answer the following question. Allow yourself 20 minutes.

■ Using the source above and your own knowledge, explain what it tells us about Roosevelt's relations with the Supreme Court.

To be able to answer questions on this topic, you will need to know about the following:

- the Treaty of Versailles as a possible cause

- weaknesses of the League of Nations
(especially after 1929)

- the impact of the Great Depression
(mass unemployment, rise of fascism)

- aggressive foreign policies of Germany, Italy and Japan in the 1930s
(collapse of the Stresa Front, Rome-Berlin Axis)

- European crises, 1934-1938
(Spain, Rhineland, Austria)

- appeasement, and reasons for it
(Britain, France)

This section deals with developments in Europe 1934-1938, focusing on:

■ European crises

■ appeasement.

This section tests you on answering short-answer questions. These normally carry relatively few marks and you need only write a few sentences. But make sure your answers are factual and focus **exactly** on the question – often just two or three facts are all that is required.

Even if the exam instructions only tell you to write one sentence, it is usually a good idea to write *two*: a sentence to give a brief explanation of the meaning of the term, and a second sentence to link it to the history connected to it. If you get into this habit, you should be able to get higher marks.

FactZONE

You need to learn these key facts.

European crises

1932-1933   Hitler took Germany out of the Disarmament Conference and the League of Nations.

1934   Hitler attempted a forced **Anschluss** (union) with Austria (against the Treaty of Versailles). Italy joined with Britain and France to prevent this.

1935   A **plebiscite** (referendum or vote) in the Saarland (a coal, iron, steel-producing region) produced a 90% majority in favour of rejoining Germany.
Hitler introduced **conscription** (compulsory military service) also against Versailles. Britain, France and Italy formed the Stresa Front to oppose Germany. BUT the Stresa Front weakened because of:

■ the Anglo-German Naval Treaty (allowing the German navy to expand to 35% of Britain's navy)
■ the Abyssinian invasion (Italy angry at the limited opposition from Britain and France).

1936   Hitler reoccupied the Rhineland (against the Treaty of Versailles).
The start of the Spanish Civil War. Italy and Germany helped Nationalists by providing weapons and troops.
The Rome-Berlin **Axis** (alliance) was signed, so breaking the Stresa Front.

1938   Hitler sent in troops to achieve Anschluss with Austria. 99% of those Austrians voting in the Nazi-run plebiscite approved the Anschluss.

Factors behind appeasement

The term **appeasement** means making concessions to aggressive countries in order to avoid war.

1931-1936

■ The USA's foreign policy was isolationist. Britain and France felt too weak to take action against aggressive countries.

■ Britain and France had different aims so were not very close. France feared to take action on its own.

■ Many felt Germany (and Italy) had reasonable grievances against the Treaty of Versailles.

■ Britain feared communism, so was not prepared to form an alliance with the Soviet Union.

■ Lack of firm opposition encouraged Hitler to further aggression.

1937-1938

■ Chamberlain became British prime minister – like many who had lived through the First World War, he was horrified at the possibility of another war.

■ Many people were against re-armament. Instead they supported the League of Nations and pacifism.

■ Like previous British prime ministers, Chamberlain wished to protect the British Empire.

■ Canada, Australia, New Zealand and South Africa said they wouldn't fight over petty European disputes.

■ Appeasement was also a policy of playing for time, to enable Britain and France to rearm.

📺 European crises

Study sources A and B below, which refer to events in Europe 1936-1938, and then answer the questions which follow.

Source A
A British cartoon of 1936 about the reoccupation of the Rhineland.

THE GOOSE-STEP.
"GOOSEY GOOSEY GANDER,
WHITHER DOST THOU WANDER?"
"ONLY THROUGH THE RHINELAND—
PRAY EXCUSE MY BLUNDER!"

Source B
Crowds welcoming German troops after the Anschluss in Austria, March 1938.

 REMEMBER Short-answer questions usually ask you to define a particular word or phrase and explain briefly its historical context, i.e. to what particular event the word or phrase is connected.

◎ *Write one or two sentences to explain the term "Rhineland" (source A). Write one or two sentences to explain the term "Anschluss'" (source B). Write one or two sentences to explain the significance of the Stresa Front in the years 1934-1938.*

Rhineland is an area of German land between the River Rhine and France. It was made a demilitarised zone (Treaty of Versailles), i.e. German troops were not allowed there.
Anschluss means union and refers to the union of Austria and Germany (forbidden by the peace treaties of Versailles and St Germain). This union extended the German border with Czechoslovakia.
Stresa Front was the alliance between Great Britain, France and Italy (1935) to oppose German expansion (Italy had helped prevent a German takeover of Austria, 1934). It weakened during 1935-1936. Italy then left, allowing the German takeover of Austria, 1938.

📺 Appeasement

Study the two sources below, which refer to the policy of appeasement in the years 1936-1938.

Source A A view expressed by Chamberlain, before becoming Prime Minister in 1937.

> War wins nothing, cures nothing, ends nothing. When I think of the 7 million young men who were cut off in their prime, the 13 million who were maimed or mutilated, the misery and suffering of the mothers and the fathers … in war there are no winners, but all are losers.

A

Source B Cartoon, criticising appeasement

"EUROPE CAN LOOK FORWARD TO A CHRISTMAS OF PEACE", SAYS HITLER

B

❗ **REMEMBER**
Don't just give an explanation of the terms.

❓ *Think about how you can use your own knowledge to add factual details to show the historical importance of the terms.*

Practise questions – appeasement

Study sources A and B above and write one or two sentences to answer each of the following questions. Allow yourself 15 minutes.

1 Explain the term "appeasement".

2 Explain the term "plebiscite".

3 Explain the importance of the USA's isolationist foreign policy.

To be able to answer questions on this topic, you will need to know about the following:

• problems in the Sudetenland (part of Czechoslovakia with 3 million German-speakers)

• Chamberlain, appeasement and the Munich Agreement (the Soviet Union was excluded from talks over the Sudeten crisis and there was great concern over the Munich Agreement)

• German invasion of the rest of Czechoslovakia

• the Pact of Steel (Germany and Italy)

• German threats to Poland

• the Nazi-Soviet Non-Aggression Pact (this was a promise not to attack each other, and it contained a secret **protocol** (clause) for the division of Poland and Soviet control of the Baltic states)

• the beginning of the Second World War ("phoney war")

This section focuses on two important events associated with the final causes of the Second World War:

■ the Munich Agreement

■ the Nazi-Soviet Non-Aggression Pact.

In this section you will practice answering short-answer questions. For this type of question you need to write a few sentences, combining definitions of important terms, or explanations of particular features of a cartoon, with factual explanations of their historical context/ significance.

Always try to write *two* sentences about each term or phrase: one to give a brief definition, and another to explain the history connected to it. That way, you should ensure you cover all the relevant points the Chief Examiner is looking for.

FactZONE

The Munich Agreement, September 1938

28 March   Hitler met Henlein, the Nazi leader of the Sudeten Germans, and ordered him to stir up trouble in the Sudetenland.

21–22 May   France and the Soviet Union reaffirmed their support for Czechoslovakia.

30 May   Hitler finalised his plans to conquer Czechoslovakia for **Lebensraum** (living space).

June–July   Tension and conflict increased in the Sudetenland. Britain and France tried to get the Czech government to make concessions.

28 August   Britain's War Minister informed Chamberlain that Britain wasn't ready for war.

15 Sept   Chamberlain met Hitler at Berchtesgaden and agreed that Hitler should have the Sudetenland.

18–21 Sept   France supported the plan and, with Britain, forced the Czechoslovak Prime Minister, Benes, to accept.

22 Sept   Chamberlain met Hitler at Bad Godesberg. Hitler made new demands for immediate occupation, and issued an **ultimatum** (final demand/threat) to the Czechs, to end on 28 September.

29 Sept   Chamberlain met Hitler at Munich (with France and Italy) and agreed to the immediate transfer of the Sudetenland to Germany.

The Nazi-Soviet Non-Aggression Pact, August 1939

1934   Germany and Poland signed a non-aggression treaty. The fear of Nazi Germany led the Soviet Union to join the League of Nations.

1935   The USSR, France and Czechoslovakia promised "mutual assistance" if attacked. **Comintern** (Communist International) called for a "popular front" in Europe to combat fascism. The Soviet Union was concerned about the British and French inaction over Abyssinia.

1936   Hitler was allowed to re-occupy the Rhineland, despite breaking the Treaty of Versailles. Britain and France did not prevent German and Italian involvement in the Spanish Civil War. Germany and Italy signed the Rome-Berlin Axis and, with Japan, the Anti-Comintern Pact. Stalin became suspicious of the appeasement policy.

1938   The German Anschluss with Austria was not opposed, despite this being against the Treaty of Versailles.

17 April 1939   The Soviet Union failed to get Britain and France to sign a formal alliance. Britain didn't even reply till the end of May. Stalin appointed Molotov as the new Foreign Minister and began secret negotiations with Nazi Germany.

12 August   The Soviet Union made a second attempt to ally with Britain and France, but Britain and France sent no senior ministers, and refused the idea of Soviet troops marching through Polish or Romanian territory. The talks ended on 21 August.

23 August   The Nazi Foreign Minister, Ribbentrop, went to Moscow. Molotov and Ribbentrop signed the **Non–Aggression Pact**.

Short-answer questions

The Munich Agreement

Study the source below which is a passage referring to the 1938 crisis over Czechoslovakia.

An extract from *The Myths of Munich*, written by the British historian A.J.P. Taylor, and published in 1969.

> "The international conference at Munich in 1938 had a practical task: to solve the problem of the three million German-speakers in Czechoslovakia and so prevent a European war. The Munich Agreement signed at the Conference succeeded in this task. The Czechoslovak territory inhabited by the three million Germans was transferred to Germany. The Germans were satisfied, there was no war."

! REMEMBER When you are asked to define or explain a term, phrase, photo or a feature in a cartoon, you must always add relevant information from your own knowledge.

◎ *Write one or two sentences to explain the reference to "three million German speakers".*
Write one or two sentences to explain the reference to "Munich Agreement".
Write one or two sentences to explain why Hitler wanted Czechoslovak territory.

The **three million German speakers** were the Sudeten Germans, former citizens of the Austrian empire, who lived in an area of Czechoslovakia known as the Sudetenland.

The **Munich Agreement** was the agreement reached by Britain, France, Italy and Germany that Germany should have the Sudetenland. The Czechs and Russians were not consulted about this.

Hitler wanted the Sudetenland for four reasons: it contained Czech border defences; it had important armaments works (Skoda); it made further expansion eastwards (Lebensraum) easier; and it was within bombing distance of Moscow.

◎ *Highlight any relevant points of information given in the source and/or in the details of its origin.*

The Nazi-Soviet Non-Aggression Pact

Study the source below, which is a cartoon giving the Russian view of the
Munich Agreement of 1938. The signpost says 'Western Europe' and 'USSR'.

НА БОЛЬШОЙ ЕВРОПЕЙСКОЙ ДОРОГЕ

Даладье. Чемберлен

ЗАПАДНАЯ ЕВРОПА   СССР

mmmлкр Iнтлкг Геринг Гоббельс

АНГЛО-ФРАНЦУЗСКИЕ «РЕГУЛИРОВЩИКИ

(?) *Consider events
before 1938, as well
as those of 1938.
Can you think of
events that might be
useful in explaining
the Soviet view?*

Practice questions – the Nazi-Soviet Non-Aggression Pact

Allow yourself 15 minutes.

1 Write one or two sentences to explain
which countries the two figures by the
signpost are meant to represent.

2 Write one or two sentences to explain why
the Soviet Union might think these people

were directing Hitler to the east, towards
the USSR.

3 Write one or two sentences to explain what
connection might exist between the Munich
Agreement and the signing of the Nazi-Soviet
Non-Aggression Pact.

To be able to answer questions on this topic, you will need to know about the following:

- invasion of Poland and the Phoney War (Sept 1939 - April 1940)

- **Blitzkrieg** (lightning war) in the West (fall of the Low Countries and France, Dunkirk)

- the Battle of Britain and the Home Front (the Blitz, evacuation, rationing)

- the North African Campaign (on 10 June 1940, Italy declared war on Britain and France – Mussolini's plan was to build a North African Empire. In August 1940, the Italian army drove British forces out of Somaliland – the next Italian war aim was to use its 240,000-strong army in Libya to drive Wavell's 36,000-strong British army from Egypt. Then on 9 December 1940, after a slow retreat, Wavell launched a successful counter-offensive against Graziani's army which had been weakened by diversion of supplies to help the faltering Italian invasion of Greece)

- Operation **Barbarossa** and the Eastern Front (the Red Army was taken by surprise. The Soviet army retreated rapidly, faced by 153 German divisions – 3 million men. Stalin ordered the **scorched earth** policy (burning crops and buildings), the use of **partisan** (guerrilla) forces, and the removal of 1500 factories eastwards away from the fighting)

- Pearl Harbour and war in the Pacific

- the War at sea (submarines, Battle of the Atlantic)

- Allied offensives (Soviet counter attacks, D-Day landings)

- defeat of the Axis powers

This section focuses on two important theatres of the Second World War:

- North Africa

- the Eastern Front.

This section tests your skills at answering questions for which you need to write one or two paragraphs. For such questions you need to explain *why* something happened, or *what* was important. They are like mini-essays and you must *think* about what you are writing, so that your answer is structured in a logical way.

FactZONE

You need to learn these key facts:

The North African Campaign

April 1941
Rommel arrived in Libya with extra troops to strengthen the **Axis** (countries who'd signed the Rome-Berlin-Tokyo Axis) forces. Rommel's **Afrika Korps** (German plus Italian troops in North Africa) soon drove the British army out of Libya.

June 1941
Churchill urged Wavell into a premature and unsuccessful offensive. Wavell was replaced by Auchinleck.

18 Nov 1941
"Operation Crusader" defeated the Afrika Korps and relieved Tobruk (7 Dec).

May 1942
Rommel's counter-attack defeated the British 8th Army and captured Tobruk.

August 1942
Montgomery took over the 8th Army.

23 Oct–4 Nov 1942
The Axis' forces were heavily defeated at El Alamein (Axis tanks were outnumbered 2:1). The Afrika Korps started to retreat.

8 Nov 1942
Anglo-American landings took place and the Afrika Korps surrendered in Tunisia.

May 1943
There were no Axis forces left in North Africa.

The Eastern Front

22 June 1941
Hitler launched Operation Barbarossa (invasion of Russia).

July–Dec 1941
The German advance began to slow down. The siege of Leningrad began in October and lasted 3 years. By December, the German army was near Moscow.

Dec 1941
The Red Army, led by Zhukov, launched a counter-offensive and saved Moscow. The Russian winter began to hit German forces (who were only equipped for a quick summer campaign).

Jan–Feb 1942
There were unsuccessful Russian counter-attacks. The Germans concentrated on the Caucasus oil fields and Stalingrad in south Russia.

Sept–Nov 1942
Von Paulus' 250,000-strong VI **Panzer** (German armoured vehicles) Army reached the suburbs of Stalingrad. Zhukov launched a successful counter-offensive.

31 Jan 1943
The Russians won the Battle of Stalingrad. Von Paulus surrendered (with only 91,000 men left). Stalin asked the Allies to open up a Second Front.

July 1943
The German offensive at Kursk (biggest tank battle in history) was defeated by the Red Army (the Soviet T34 tank was superior).

Sept 1943–Jan 1944
The Russians were on the offensive. They recaptured Smolensk, Kiev and ended the siege of Leningrad.

By August 1944, all German troops had been expelled from Russia. In all, 75% of all German troops and war material were deployed on the Russian (Eastern) Front.

One– or two-paragraph answers

The North African campaign

Study the source below, which shows British tanks at El Alamein in 1942.

 REMEMBER
For such questions don't just describe something. To get high marks, you need to show historical understanding, by using your knowledge to explain the causes or the importance of something.

◎ *Write one or two paragraphs to explain why Rommel's Afrika Korps reinforcements were sent in 1941.*

Write one or two paragraphs to explain the significance of the battle of El Alamein.

Italian forces under Graziani were being defeated. Their supplies were running short because they had been diverted to Greece.
North Africa and the Mediterranean Sea were important for oil and trade routes (Egypt and the Suez Canal). So it was vital for the Axis powers to defeat Britain.

El Alamein was a decisive victory. The Afrika Korps were forced to retreat. This allowed Anglo-US troop landings in North Africa. The Axis forces in North Africa surrendered, and the Allies were able to begin the invasion of Italy.

The Eastern Front

Study the source below, which is a map showing the progress of Operation Barbarossa, June–December 1941.

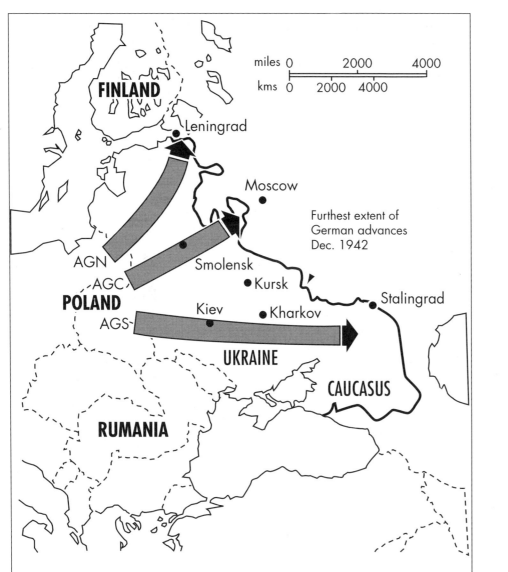

KEY

AGN = Army Group North

AGC = Army Group Central

AGS = Army Group South

! REMEMBER Don't just describe what happened. Focus clearly on what the questions ask.

(?) *Think how you can use your knowledge to explain why there were problems with Operation Barbarossa and why the battle of Stalingrad was important.*

Practice questions – the Eastern Front

Use the source and your own knowledge to write one or two paragraphs to answer each of the following questions. Allow yourself 20 minutes.

1 Explain why Operation Barbarossa had not been successful by December 1941.

2 Explain the importance of the battle of Stalingrad in the winter of 1942–1943.

Conferences 1943–1945

To be able to answer questions on this topic, you will need to know about the following:

- the Eastern Front and Stalin's call for a Second Front

- the Tehran Conference, November 1943

- Red Army victories, 1944

- the D Day Landings (the Second Front)

- the Yalta Conference, February 1945

- the death of Roosevelt - Vice-President Truman takes over in the USA

- the Potsdam Conference, July - August 1945

- the USA and the atomic bomb

This section deals with the Allied Conferences 1943-1945, focusing on:

- the Tehran Conference
- the Potsdam Conference.

This section tests your ability to answer causation or *why* questions, as a lead-in to writing a full essay. Remember that for such questions you don't just *describe* events – you must use the facts to *explain why* something happened, or why something was important.

Because they are like mini-essays, it is important that you write in a planned and logical way – so it might be useful to make a rough list of points/events first, *before* you begin to write your final answer.

FactZONE

You need to learn these key facts:

Conferences, 1943-1945

Conferences	Points agreed	Points not agreed/carried out
Tehran, November 1943 (Stalin–USSR, Roosevelt–USA, Churchill–GB) (War still raging on Eastern Front)	Britain and the USA to open up a Second Front in France.	Objections by Churchill delayed the Second Front until June 1944.
	USSR to declare war on Japan after defeat of Germany.	
	USSR to keep eastern Poland. Poland to be compensated with land from Germany.	
	Germany to be divided up between USSR, USA and Britain (later extended to include France), and principle accepted that Germany should pay reparations.	No details were worked out.
Potsdam July–August 1945 (Stalin–USSR, Truman–USA, Churchill/Attlee–GB) (Germany defeated, and USA about to drop atomic bombs on Japan)	Nazi party to be banned and war criminals to be put on trial.	
	The border between Poland and Germany was settled, along the rivers Oder and Neisse.	
	Germany to be divided temporarily into 4 Allied zones.	No decision was taken about long-term future of Germany.
	Each power to take reparations from its own zone. USSR also to have 25% of industrial equipment from other zones.	The Soviet zone was mainly agricultural, and little equipment was handed over from western zones.
		The USA blocked USSR from sharing in the running of Germany's rich industrial area of the Ruhr.
		The USA blocked USSR from sharing in the occupation of Japan.
		USSR prevent the USA and Britain from having influence in Eastern Europe.

Causation or "why" questions

The Tehran Conference

Read the source below, which is an extract about the war in Russia from a history book published in Britain in 1987.

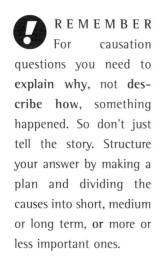

> **REMEMBER**
> For causation questions you need to **explain why**, not **describe how**, something happened. So don't just tell the story. Structure your answer by making a plan and dividing the causes into short, medium or long term, **or** more or less important ones.

The war in Russia was crucial to the Allied victory. At least 75% of Germany's troops and war material had been sent to the Russian front, which in June 1944 tied down 228 German and Axis divisions (some 4 million men) and 5250 tanks. German divisions in Western Europe at this time totalled just 61.

> **REMEMBER**
> Divide the causes /reasons into longer and shorter-term ones, and develop each point into a paragraph.

◎ *Why was Stalin suspicious about the Second Front not being opened up until June 1944?*

Longer term:
- ■ The hostility between capitalism and communism, and USA and British involvement in Russia's Civil War, 1918-1920.
- ■ The appeasement of Nazi Germany, and rejection of Stalin's offers of an anti-Nazi alliance, 1936-1939.

Shorter term:
- ■ Extent and bitterness of fighting on the Eastern Front - Soviet losses were immense.
- ■ The Second Front promised at Tehran in November 1943, but nothing happened until June 1944.

> **REMEMBER**
> Use your knowledge about the Tehran Conference and knowledge of previous history.

⑰ The Potsdam Conference

Study the source below, which shows the number of lives lost by various countries in the Second World War.

	Soldiers	Civilians
Australia	29,295	243
Britain	271,311	95,297
Canada	39,319	not known
France	205,000	173,000
Germany	3,300,000	800,000
India	36,092	79,498
Japan	1,380,000	933,000
Italy	279,820	93,000
USSR	13,600,000	7,720,000
USA	292,131	5,662

⁇ *Think about how you can discuss the effects of the Second World War on the Soviet Union and their significance.*

⁇ *Can you make a list of 4 or 5 points about the wartime conferences which could then become the basis of your paragraphs?*

❗ REMEMBER For the question below, sort the reasons according to time-scale **and/or** importance. Deal with all three wartime Allied conferences.

Practice question – the Potsdam conference

Write four or five paragraphs to answer this question. Allow yourself 30 minutes.

■ Why was Stalin likely to be dissatisfied with the outcome of the Potsdam Conference?

To be able to answer questions on this topic, you will need to know about the following:

• the closing stages of the Second World War (especially the Red Army's drive through Eastern Europe to Germany, 1944-1945)

• the wartime conferences (especially Yalta and Potsdam)

• wartime devastation of the USSR (the Soviet Union was considerably weakened after the Second World War with 25 million dead and much industry destroyed)

• the Soviet Union's possible motives and fears: invasion via Poland, as in 1914 and 1941, the revival of Germany, (the desire for a "buffer zone"), US atomic bomb

• stages of the Soviet take-over (establishment of "satellite" states)

This section deals with the Soviet Union's take-over of Eastern Europe, 1945-1948, focusing on:

■ Soviet motives

■ Poland.

This section tests your skills at answering questions which ask you to consider the usefulness of sources. Remember that all sources, even biased ones, can be useful. Also, don't forget to say something about the origin of the sources (who wrote it, when, why).

You need to learn these key facts:

Soviet motives

■ the Soviet Union feared future invasion via Eastern European states. Before the war, Poland, Hungary, Romania and Bulgaria had been ruled by right-wing governments hostile to the USSR, and in 1920 Poland had invaded Russia.

■ Hungary, Romania and Bulgaria had been allies of Nazi Germany and the Soviet Union was determined to get **reparations** (compensation) from them.

■ the Soviet Union feared the future revival of Germany since it had invaded Russia twice already (in 1914 and 1941).

■ the Soviet Union distrusted its capitalist Allies, especially the USA which was seen as having **imperialist** ambitions (wanting to dominate the world with its great economic and military power.)

■ the Soviet Union believed it had a right to determine the future shape of Europe - of all the Allies it had made the greatest sacrifices. 80% - 10 million - of German losses had been on the Eastern Front. The Red Army had freed these countries from German control.

■ the Soviet Union distrusted the US President, Truman, and felt extremely vulnerable as the USA had the atomic bomb and refused to share the technology with the USSR.

■ the Soviet Union was therefore determined to protect itself with friendly/loyal states and form a "buffer zone" in order to prevent a future invasion and total economic domination by capitalism/US imperialism.

Poland

Feb 1945 Yalta Conference faced difficulties over the future government of Poland. Britain and USA supported the **London Poles** (government-in-exile in London) led by Mikolaczyk. These were mainly Catholics and landowners, and hostile to USSR. The Soviet Union supported the **Lublin Poles** (provisional government in Lublin, Poland). These were mostly communists, and friendly to USSR. Stalin finally agreed to form a coalition government by including some London Poles in the Lublin government and to hold free elections.

March 1945 USA and USSR disagreed about the extent of future role of the London Poles in Poland's government.

April 1945 Truman became President of the USA and bigger differences emerged at the Potsdam Conference.

June 1945 A few London Poles finally joined the communist-dominated government.

July 1945 This government was **recognised** (officially accepted) by Britain and USA.

March 1946 The Pro-Communist National Front coalition party won 90% of the votes, and formed a pro-communist government. The main opposition to communists came from Mikolaczyk's Peasant Party.

January 1947 The elections were rigged. Mikolaczyk and other leaders opposed to communists fled to the West and the National Front absorbed the Peasant Party to form the Polish Communist Party.

Examining sources for usefulness

Soviet motives

Study the source below which is a French cartoon which shows Stalin attempting to spread communism throughout Europe after 1945.

The text says: "Caucasian dance" and names Eastern European countries - Poland, Bulgaria, Hungary, Czechoslovakia, Romania, the Baltic States, and both parts of Germany, as well as China and France.

> ❶ **REMEMBER** Even a clearly biased source is useful. You must use your own historical knowledge to explain **why** it is biased. Use any information supplied by the examiner about the source.

> ❶ **REMEMBER** To get high marks you must comment on the **author** (e.g. was he/she in a position to know?), the **nature** of the source, and its possible **purpose**.

◎ *How useful is the source as historical evidence about the Soviet take-over of Eastern Europe after the Second World War?*

The source is useful in that it gives some factually correct information (Stalin was leader of USSR); and references to the take-over of countries are accurate (apart from China and designs on France).

The source is not useful in that it doesn't explain motives, only actions. Also it is biased (France is an ally of Britain and USA) as it gives only a Western view; it is likely to be influenced by the developing Cold War.

◎ *Highlight any information provided in the source and/or in the details of its origin.*

 # Poland

Read the source below, which is an explanation of Soviet concerns about the future government of Poland made by Stalin in a speech at the Yalta Conference.

REMEMBER
Use any information about the source provided by the examiner.

> Mr Churchill has said that for Great Britain the Polish question is one of honour. But for the Russians it is a question both of honour and security. Throughout history Poland has been the corridor of attacks on Russia. It is not merely a question of honour for Russia, but one of life and death.

Extract from a speech by Stalin at the Yalta Conference, February 1945

REMEMBER
Even a biased sentence can be useful.

(?) *Think about whether the source is likely to be biased.*

(?) *Consider the author, nature and possible purpose/motive of the source. How can you use your own knowledge to discuss the accuracy or inaccuracy of the information, and what the source doesn't tell us?*

(◎) *Highlight any information on the source, and/or in the origin details.*

Practice question – Poland

Use the source above and your own knowledge to write two paragraphs to answer the question. Allow yourself 20 minutes.

■ How useful is this source as historical evidence of the reasons for the Soviet Union's take-over of Poland in the years 1945–1947?

To be able to answer questions on this topic, you will need to know about the following:

- the breakdown of wartime trust and alliances

- the Yalta and Potsdam Conferences, 1945

- Soviet take-over of Eastern Europe (the "**Iron Curtain**")

- European economies (in ruin at the end of the Second World War)

- Western fears of spread of communism (policy of **containment**) – in France, Italy and Greece, communist parties were quite popular as a result of their resistance roles.

- the US response, 1947 (**Truman Doctrine** and the **Marshall Plan**)

- the Berlin Blockade and Airlift, 1948-1949

- the Soviet response (Communist Information Bureau or COMINFORM, 1947, and Council for Mutual Economic Aid or COMECON, 1949)

- the formation of **NATO**, 1949

- the creation of West and East Germany, 1949

- the formation of the **Warsaw Pact**, 1955

❗ REMEMBER
With history questions, there is usually more than one side to the answer. Make sure you cover both supporting and opposing information.

This section deals with the beginnings of the Cold War 1945-1949, focusing on:

- the Marshall Plan
- formation of NATO.

It also gives you practice at answering interpretation questions based on sources and your own knowledge. These questions present you with a particular view of an aspect of history, and then ask you to comment on that view.

You need to learn these key facts:

The Marshall Plan, 1947

March 1946   Churchill made his "Iron Curtain" speech in the USA, as the Soviet Union's control of Eastern Europe began.

April 1946   Council of Foreign Ministers – USA blocked all Soviet proposals and condemned their actions in Eastern Europe.

Jan 1947   Many parts of Europe suffered economic crisis (unemployment) and food shortages (bad harvests, 1946). Support for communists was growing in France and Italy.

Feb 1947   Britain told USA it could no longer afford to support the Greek royalists in civil war against the Greek communists.

March 1947   President Truman announced his intention to **contain** (stop) the spread of communism, with economic and military aid. This became known as the Truman Doctrine (part of what became the Domino Theory).

June 1947   USA announced massive economic aid for Europe, under the direction of George Marshall – usually known as Marshall Aid or the Marshall Plan. The idea was to rebuild economies to prevent the spread of communism. This aid was not available to Eastern Europe, unless American capitalist methods were adopted. Stalin stopped Eastern European countries applying for such aid.

1952   Marshall Plan ended. During its four years, 1947-1951, the USA gave $13 billion, spent according to an Economic Recovery Programme (ERP) drawn up by Western European countries (in the summer of 1946). European economy had much improved by 1952, as had US exports to Europe.

Formation of NATO, 1949

1945   The Soviet Union began to establish control of Eastern European **satellite** (client or subordinate) states.

March 1946   Churchill made his "Iron Curtain" speech.

Jan-June 1947   Economic crisis in Europe, and civil war in Greece, led to the Truman Doctrine and Marshall Plan, to prevent/contain spread of communism. Britain and US merged their zones in Germany (known as **Bizonia**).

October 1947   The USSR set up Cominform to increase its control of Eastern Europe.

March 1948   Communists took control in Czechoslovakia. Western European countries formed the Brussels Treaty Organisation (BTO).

June 1948   France merged its zone in Germany with Bizonia to form **Trizonia**. A new currency, the Deutschmark, was introduced. The Soviet authorities began the Berlin Blockade, fearing revival of Germany. The Allies responded with the Berlin Airlift.

April 1949   BTO became the North Atlantic Treaty Organisation (NATO) with the USA and Canada as new members, the USA being the strongest partner.

Interpretation questions

📺 The Marshall Plan 1947

Study the two sources below, which relate to the Marshall Plan.

Source A A comment made by President Truman.

> "*The Truman Doctrine and the Marshall Plan were always two halves of the same walnut*". **A**

❗ REMEMBER
When answering interpretation questions you must examine the sources **and** use your own knowledge to put forward arguments which support **and** arguments which disagree with the view given in the question.

Source B A Soviet Union cartoon attacking the Marshall Plan as an attempt at US world domination.

— Спасибо высоким господам, поддерживают меня, старуху, кто чем может!

❗ REMEMBER
Whether you agree or disagree with the view given in the question, you will need to devote about half your answer to putting forward the opposite case.

⊙ *"The Marshall Plan was part of an American plan to dominate Europe."
Using the sources and your own knowledge, write three or four paragraphs assessing the accuracy of this view.*

This view is **accurate** because:
- US economy needed a prosperous Europe
- Europe was likely to become dependent on US aid
- it went hand in hand with the political and military power of USA (NATO).

This view is **inaccurate** because:
- it was a genuine attempt to relieve post-war suffering and problems
- European countries decided how to spend the money aid (ERP), not the USA
- it can be seen as preventing communist domination of all of Europe, so ensuring the freedom of Western Europe.

📺 The Formation of NATO

Study the two sources below, which comment on the formation of NATO.

Source A Extract from a speech by Britain's Foreign Minister, Ernest Bevin, in 1949, on the formation of NATO.

A

Like others, my country has had forced upon it the task of fighting two world wars against aggression within a quarter of a century. Today will bring a feeling of relief. At last democracy is no longer a series of isolated units.

B

The North Atlantic Treaty has nothing in common with the aims of self-defence of the states, who are threatened by no-one and whom no-one intends to attack. On the contrary, the Treaty has an aggressive characteristic and is aimed against the USSR.

Source B The view of the Soviet government on the establishment of NATO in 1949.

❗ REMEMBER Use **both** sources – if you only comment on one source, you will automatically lose half the marks available.

❔ *Think how you can give a balanced answer by providing facts and arguments for **and** against the statement.*

❔ *Think carefully about how to use relevant bits of your own knowledge to add to any information provided by the sources.*

Practice question – the formation of NATO

Allow yourself 20 minutes.

■ "NATO was an entirely defensive alliance, and was neither an attempt to impose US supremacy, nor a threat to the Soviet Union".

Using the sources, and your own knowledge, write three or four paragraphs assessing the accuracy of this view.

To be able to answer questions on this topic, you will need to know about the following:

• the Berlin Blockade and Airlift, 1948-1949

• the Hungarian Uprising, 1956

• the U2 Incident, 1960

• the Berlin Wall, 1961 (1945: Allied Conferences – Yalta and Potsdam – led to the division of Germany and Berlin into 4 zones – Berlin in Soviet zone. 1945-1948: the Cold War developed between the USA and the USSR – atom bomb, Eastern Europe, Truman Doctrine, Marshall Plan. 1949-1955: Cold War alliances were formed – NATO and Warsaw Pact)

• Czechoslovakia, 1968 (1948: the Communists took power in Czechoslovakia – part of Soviet control of Eastern Europe. 1949-1955: the Cold War developed and opposing alliances were formed – NATO and Warsaw Pact)

This section deals with the Cold War in Europe in the 1960s, focusing on:

■ the Berlin Wall, 1961

■ Czechoslovakia, 1968.

This section tests your ability to answer causation (or why) essay questions. For this type of question you need to do more than just tell the story. You must point out the various causes. Do a rough plan first, sorting out your causes according to time-scale (long, medium or short) and/or relative importance. Include a summary at the beginning or end.

Don't just describe a series of events – try to come to a *judgement* about which cause(s) you think was/were most important, in your final paragraph. If you try to do this, it should help you avoid writing a purely descriptive essay.

The Berlin Wall, 1961

1956 Khrushchev (USSR) announced the policy of "peaceful coexistence" with the West. This was the start of the "Thaw" in the Cold War.

1958 Khrushchev called for an end to the 4-power control of Berlin. Nearly 3 million East Germans (mainly educated/skilled) had **defected** (fled) to the more prosperous West Berlin between 1949 and 1960. West Berlin was also the headquarters for Western spying networks.

Sept 1959 Eisenhower (USA) met with Khrushchev at Camp David and indicated that concessions on Berlin were possible.

May 1960 The Soviet Union shot down a US spy plane (U2) flying over the USSR. Eisenhower refused to apologise. The pilot (Gary Powers) was put on trial. The Paris **Summit** (meeting) over the Berlin question broke up and the "Thaw" ended.

Nov 1960 Kennedy elected US President. He was less prepared to compromise with the Soviet Union.

June 1961 At the Vienna Summit, Khrushchev's demand for a neutral Berlin was refused. The USSR increased its military spending.

July 1961 The USA publicly rejected all Soviet demands and increased its military strength in Western Europe.

August 1961 The uncertainty over the future of Berlin meant there were more defectors to West Berlin, rising to almost 1000 a day. The East Germans erected barricades to seal off East Berlin. Later, the stone Berlin Wall was built.

Czechoslovakia, 1968

1956 There was a revolt in Poland and the Hungarian Uprising took place. The Soviet Union invaded Hungary because it feared the Warsaw Pact might break up. There was no unrest in Czechoslovakia, ruled since 1953 by Novotny (secretary of Communist Party and President).

Oct-Dec 1967 Opposition grew to Novotny within the Czech Communist Party. Brezhnev (USSR) visited Prague.

Jan 1968 Alexander Dubcek became leader of the Czech Communist Party.

Mar-Apr 1968 Novotny resigned as President. Dubcek began the **Prague Spring** - "socialism with a human face". These were a series of liberal reforms (lifting of censorship, freedom to travel, toleration of religions). In order to revive the economy, the government also developed trade with the West, but made no plans to leave the Warsaw Pact.

May-June 1968 There was growing concern in the USSR and some Warsaw Pact countries (especially East Germany) about the impact and direction of Dubcek's reforms.

July 1968 Warsaw Letter criticised Dubcek's policies.

August 1968 Tito (leader of non-Warsaw Pact communist Yugoslavia) visited Prague; then Dubcek signed a pact with Romania (Romania was also in disagreement with the USSR). Brezhnev feared Czechoslovakia was about to leave the Warsaw Pact, opening up USSR's defences against West Germany. Warsaw Pact armies invaded. Dubcek was removed from power.

Causation essays

REMEMBER
For causation essays – always make a plan. Don't just describe **what** happened, explain **why** it happened. Then summarise in an opening or concluding paragraph.

The Berlin Wall 1961

Study the two sources below, which relate to the crisis over Berlin in 1961.

Source A
Map showing the Berlin Wall, and East and West Germany.

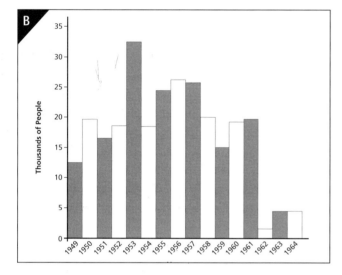

Source B
Chart showing the number of defectors from East to West Germany, 1949-1964.

◎ *Using these sources and your own knowledge, explain why the Berlin Wall was built in 1961.*

REMEMBER
Identify several different causes or factors. If possible, set these out according to a time-scale (long, medium and short term). Show which you think are **more** important and which are **less** important.

For this question the causes can be divided into long, medium and short term, as follows.

Long term: (1945-1955)	■ breakdown of wartime alliances ■ emergence of Cold War (fears and suspicions) ■ specific Soviet concerns over Germany and Berlin (1948-49 Berlin Blockade and Airlift)
Medium term: (1956-1960)	■ Khrushchev and Eisenhower - the "Thaw" ■ problems of spies and defectors to West Berlin ■ breakdown of the "Thaw" (U2 Incident)
Short term: (1960-1961)	■ Kennedy becomes President of USA ■ increasing tension and defections

Check your textbook for any additional information.

📺 Czechoslovakia 1968

Study the two sources below, which relate to Czechoslovakia in 1968.

A

Twice this century the Russians have had to face an attack from the centre of Europe. Only they know the extent of their losses in the last war ... and the country is still governed by the men who fought in it. The Russians have no intention of pulling down their defences in the west.

Source A
Extract on events in Czechoslovakia in 1968 written by a Czech historian, published in 1972.

❗ **R E M E M B E R** Do a rough plan first. Sort your reasons according to time and/or importance. Write a concluding paragraph to sum up the arguments.

Source B
Map showing Czechoslovakia and its neighbours.

🤔 *Think about the significance of the phrase "Warsaw Pact forces". Try to comment on the possible motives of the other members of the Warsaw pact, not just the Soviet Union.*

Practice question - Czechoslovakia

Write three or four paragraphs to answer the following question. Allow yourself 30 minutes.

■ Using sources A and B and your own knowledge, explain why Warsaw Pact troops marched into Czechoslovakia in 1968.

To be able to answer questions about this topic, you will need to know something about the following:

• the Korean War, 1950-1953 (1945: at the end of the Second World War, Korea was divided along the 38th parallel, with Russian troops in the North and US troops in the South. 1948: separate governments were set up; North – communist, South – capitalist as a result of the Cold War. 1949: Mao Zedong and the Chinese Communist Party came to power in China – Truman Doctrine, containment, "Domino Theory". The Soviet Union exploded its first atom bomb.)

• the Suez Crisis, 1956

• the Cuban Missile Crisis, 1962

• the Vietnam War, 1961-1975 (1945: Vietnam – part of the French colony of Indo-China – was liberated from the Japanese, and handed back to France. 1946-1954: Vietnamese nationalists and communists – led by Ho Chi Minh – fought against French rule. The USA gave aid to the French – "Domino Theory". 1954: the French were defeated at Dien Bien Phu. They withdrew, and Vietnam was divided into North – communist – and South – capitalist, – along the 17th parallel, by the Geneva Conference. 1955-1960: the USA gave aid to South Vietnam, after Southern communists – Vietcong – began a guerrilla war in South Vietnam because elections aimed at reunifying the country, promised at Geneva for 1956, failed to take place. North Vietnam backed the Vietcong.)

• the Six-Day War, 1967

• détente

This section deals with aspects of the Cold War in Asia, focusing on

■ the Korean War

■ the Vietnam War.

This section tests your ability to answer questions which focus on the usefulness of sources. Remember, even if the source is biased, it can still be useful as historical evidence e.g. as an example of propaganda, or of a view held by certain groups or individuals.

Korean War, 1950-1953

April 1950 The government in South Korea was very unpopular. Many voted in the South for unification with North Korea. There were clashes between North and South armies.

June 1950 North Korea invaded South Korea to reunite Korea by force. It conquered all but the Pusan area.

July 1950 The USA sent troops under General MacArthur to help South Korea. It persuaded the UN to send troops as well. (The USSR was boycotting the Security Council, so was unable to **veto** (stop) this decision.) The USSR sent weapons, but no troops, to the North.

Sept 1950 USA launched successful counter-attack at Inchon and Pusan.

1 Oct 1950 US troops reached 38th parallel (border between North and South Korea).

7 Oct 1950 MacArthur was authorised by Truman to invade North Korea and soon reached the Yalu River, close to the Chinese border.

10 Oct 1950 The Chinese government warned the USA not to come nearer to their border. The USA ignored China and on 26 October China sent 300,000 troops to help North Korea.

Nov 1950 US and South Korean troops were forced to retreat by the Chinese forces.

1 Jan 1951 Chinese troops crossed the 38th parallel. Truman and MacArthur considered using atomic bombs on China. The British government opposed this.

Feb-March 1951 US counter-attack pushed communist forces back to the 38th parallel. MacArthur was dismissed for criticising Truman's new policy of doing a deal with China.

April-May 1951 A Chinese counter-attack was unsuccessful and stalemate was reached.

July 1951-Dec 1952 Peace talks took place but there was no ceasefire.

Jan-July 1953 The new USA president, Eisenhower, finally negotiated a ceasefire. Korea remained divided, as no final agreement was reached.

The Vietnam War, 1961-1975

1961-1963 Kennedy decided to send military advisers to help South Vietnam. Later, he sent special troops to help South Vietnam against the Vietcong.

1964-1968 President Johnson **escalated** (greatly increased) US involvement. After 3 years, 540,000 US troops were in South Vietnam.
The Gulf of Tonkin Incident (1964) was used to justify Operation Rolling Thunder (1965) - the bombing of Ho Chi Minh Trail supply routes and North Vietnam.
The Tet Offensive and My-Lai massacre (1968) increased opposition to war in the USA, as did the use of napalm and Agent Orange (a **defoliant** - a chemical preparation for stripping leaves).

1969-1973 Nixon, the new US President, sought a way to end US involvement ('Vietnamisation' = leaving war to the South Vietnam's army), but also extended US bombing, to Laos and Cambodia. Ceasefire was signed in 1973 in Paris and US forces pulled out.

1973-1975 Fighting between North and South ended in victory for the North and reunification.

The Korean War

Study the two sources below, which are about the Korean War.

Source A
An illustration of the "Domino Theory".

VIETNAM, 1961 · KOREA, 1950 · CHINA, 1949 · EAST GERMANY, 1949 · CZECHOSLOVAKIA, 1948 · HUNGARY, 1947 · ROMANIA, 1946 · BULGARIA, 1946 · POLAND, 1945

A

Source B
Extract from a speech by the US President, in 1950, after the invasion of South Korea by North Korea.

> ...The attack upon Korea makes it plain beyond all doubt that Communism has passed beyond the use of subversion to conquer independent nations and will now use armed invasion and war.

B

> **!** **R E M E M B E R**
> No source is completely useless, even if it is biased. Make sure you deal with the usefulness of **all** sources referred to in the question – many candidates lose marks simply because they only write about one source.

> **!** **R E M E M B E R**
> To assess fully a source's usefulness, consider:
>
> ■ is the information accurate? (Use your own knowledge about the topic.)
>
> ■ who produced the source? why? when? (remember to look for **and** use any information provided by the examiner about the source.)

(?) *How useful are Sources A and B as historical evidence of US motives and policies in the Korean War?*

Useful because:
■ Source A refers to the Domino Theory - related to the Truman Doctrine (1947). Dates of Soviet takeover of Eastern Europe correct.
■ Source B - from US President (so should know) - ties in with Source A and policy of containment.

Problems:
■ The sources only show motives for involvement in 1950 - objectives changed (from saving South, to overthrowing North) 1951-1953
■ Would a US President in the Cold War publicly reveal all motives? What is the purpose of Source B?

⊙ *Highlight the information in the sources and/or in their origin details.*

The Vietnam War

Study Sources A and B below, which are about opposition in the USA to the continued involvement in the Vietnam War.

Source A
US Cartoon, 1965.

'Just give us the tools and we'll get the job done.'

Source B
Murdered civilians at My-Lai, Vietnam, 1968, published 1969.

◎ *Highlight the information given in the sources and/or in their origin details.*

! **REMEMBER**
Say what is useful **and** what is not so useful about **both** sources.

? *Is the information or viewpoint accurate? Is it complete? Is it biased? Are there any important aspects we are not told about?*

Practice question – the Vietnam war

Use sources A and B above to write two or three paragraphs to answer the following question. Allow yourself 20 minutes.

■ How useful are sources A and B as historical evidence about why the US was forced to withdraw from the Vietnam War in 1973?

The First World War 1914–1919

Armistice
ceasefire – the end of the First World War fighting

Conscientious objectors
people who refused to join the army on moral or religious grounds, sometimes called "conchies"

Conscription
when people are forced by law to join the armed services, and possibly imprisoned if they refuse

Convoy system
merchant ships sailing together in a zig-zag pattern protected by destroyers

Going over the top
troops advancing out of their trenches en masse

Hydrophones
equipment used to detect submarines

No-man's land
ground between two opposing front lines, controlled by neither side

Propaganda
use of the media through songs, newspapers, posters etc. to put forward a particular point of view

Race for the sea
race to capture the Channel ports in the First World War

Reserved occupations
jobs that were exempt from conscription, such as miners, farmers etc.

U-boats
German submarines

War of attrition
to win by destroying more enemy forces, whatever the losses of one's own troops, and so wear down the other side

Zeppelins
German airships used to bomb British cities in the First World War

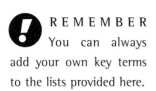

REMEMBER
You can always add your own key terms to the lists provided here.

International Relations 1919–1939

Articles of the Covenant
rules that governed the League of Nations

Isolationism
policy of non-involvement in world affairs practised by the USA between the First and Second World Wars

League of Nations
formed after the First World War to help prevent another World War, similar to the United Nations

November Criminals
name given by ordinary Germans to German politicians who signed the armistice in 1918, and the subsequent Versailles peace treaty in 1919

Reparations
compensation money Germany had to pay for "causing" the First World War

The Big Three
victors of the First World War – the USA, France and Britain

Treaty of Versailles
signed at the end of the First World War between the Allies and Germany

War Guilt Clause
the part of the Versailles Treaty in which Germany accepted responsibilty for starting the First World War

Russia in Revolution 1917–1941

Bolsheviks
group of Russian revolutionaries led by Lenin who gained power in 1917

Commissar
title given to ministers in the revolutionary Bolshevik government

Collectivisation
system in which small private farms were merged into larger state farms

Five-Year Plans
drawn up under Stalin to speed up industrialisation of the USSR

Kulaks
better-off peasants

NEP
New Economic Policy – Lenin's economic reforms to ensure food supply after failure of War Communism

Purges
murder or imprisonment by Stalin of leading Bolsheviks and many millions of officials and army officers

Red army
the Bolshevik army

Show trials
trials based on little or no evidence designed to convict leading Bolsheviks, during Stalin's rule

War Communism
emergency economic measures carried out by Bolsheviks 1917–1921

White armies
anti-Bolsheviks supported by foreign powers

Germany 1919–1945

Aryan
a white person of non-Jewish descent

Chancellor
head of the German government

Depression
high unemployment and mass hardship

Final Solution
Nazi policy to wipe out the Jewish race in Europe

Hyper-inflation
vast increase in the cost of living due to the devaluation of the mark

Kristallnacht
Crystal Night, or Night of the Broken Glass, when thousands of Jewish businesses were destroyed

Nazi
a member of the National Socialist party, led by Hitler

Night of the Long Knives
purge of the S. A. (Brown shirts) by Hitler

Putsch
sudden attempt to remove a government by force

The USA 1919–1945

Buying on the margin
buying shares by paying a 10% deposit and being given credit for the rest

Federal
central (e.g. federal government)

HP
hire purchase

Laissez-faire
letting businesses operate with no government controls

Lame duck months
the time when the new president had been elected, but had not yet taken office

Rugged individualism
people helping themselves without government assistance

Supreme Court
the highest court in the US

Tariff
import duty

The Second World War 1939–1945

Anschluss
union (particularly in relation to Germany's union with Austria)

Appeasement
making concessions to aggressive countries to avoid war

Axis
the alliance between a number of fascist states in the lead-up to the Second World War

Blitzkrieg
lightning war

Comintern
Communist International

Lebensraum
a German term that means "living space"

Partisan
guerrilla

Phoney war
first few months of the Second World War when no aggressive acts by either side took place

Plebiscite
referendum or vote of the people on a particular issue

Scorched earth policy
policy of burning crops and buildings in order to deny supplies to an enemy

Ultimatum
final demand or threat

Superpower relations since 1945

Cold War
the rivalry and tension between the capitalist West and communist East after the Second World War

Contain
stop

Defect
flee to another country

Domino Theory
American theory that if one country became communist, its neighbours would follow suit

Imperialist
wanting to dominate the world with economic and military power

Iron Curtain
imaginary line between communist Eastern Europe and capitalist Western Europe

London Poles
Polish government-in-exile in London (pro-capitalist)

Lublin Poles
provisional government in Lublin, Poland (pro-communist)

Marshall Plan
American economic plan for the reconstruction of Europe after the Second World War

Reparations
compensation

Satellite
client or subordinate (e.g. satellite state)

Summit
meeting

Veto
block or prevent

Warsaw Pact
treaty between communist European countries